A GONDOLA ON THE MURRAY

A FEAST BY THE RIVER

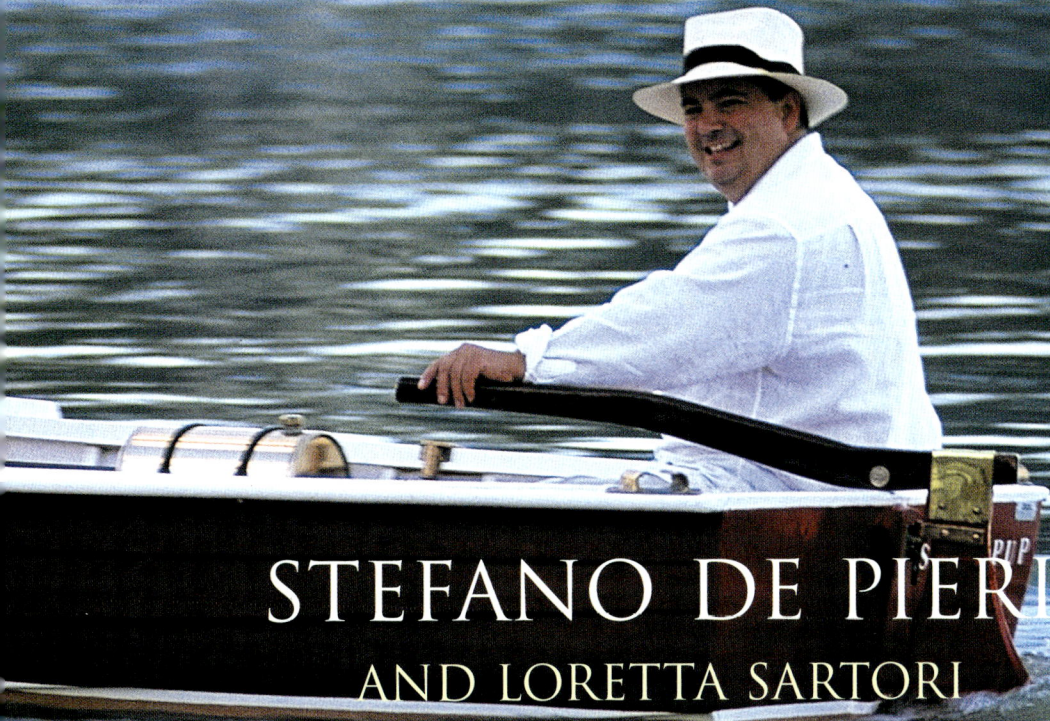

STEFANO DE PIERI

AND LORETTA SARTORI

PHOTOGRAPHS BY JOHN HAY

ABC
BOOKS

The author and publisher gratefully acknowledge the following for their kind permission to reproduce poems in this book:
Mark O'Connor c/- Curtis Brown (Aust) Pty Ltd for 'To Kill an Olive' and 'Westward Waters'
Les Murray c/- Margaret Connolly and Associates for 'Oasis City'

Published by ABC Books for the
AUSTRALIAN BROADCASTING CORPORATION
GPO Box 9994 Sydney NSW 2001

National Library of Australia
Cataloguing-in-Publication entry:
De Pieri. Stefano.
A gondola on the Murray : a feast by the river.
Includes index.
ISBN 0 7333 0865 1.
1. Cookery, Australian. 2. Australians - Food. 3. Cookery,
Italian. I. Sartori. Loretta. II. Hay. John. III. Australian
Broadcasting Corporation. IV. Title. (Series: A gondola on the Murray).
641.5994

Cover design by Reno Design
Photography by John Hay
Set in 10.5/12 Proforma Light by Seymour Designs
Film separations by PageSet, Victoria
Printed in Singapore by Tien Wah Press

5 4 3 2 1

CONTENTS

ACKNOWLEDGMENTS

To Donata, Domenico and Claudia, and all the family from Buronga to Gol Gol.

Special thanks to the team at Stefano's: Michael Stonehouse, Sarah Page, Rosalie Langdon, Kirsten Csibra, Line Carrazza, Tricia Hennessy, Kristen Penny. Also thanks to Mark O'Connor, Les Murray, Foong Ling Kong, Gianni Grigoletto, Tony Tan and staff at the Grand Hotel.

SdP

In order to have completed this book I wish to acknowledge the people who have supported me with their encouragement and assistance at Distorta. They have experienced and weathered the mayhem I dished out under the guise of 'creativity'. Thank you Marilyn Nagy Juhasz, Luke Morgan, Astrid Waclawik and Zoi Condos.

Otterino Pace gave willingly of his time and expansive knowledge to finetune the 'authenticity' and is also responsible for sewing the first seeds of my career.

Family, friends and students selflessly consumed the test recipes, responding with constructive criticism through to verbal abuse for the extra grams they were carrying.

I must also acknowledge Tony Tan, not only for introducing me to Stefano, but also for his continued faith in my work.

Thank you.

LS

INTRODUCTION

The book and the television series, *Gondola on the Murray*, were so well received I feel encouraged and justified to pursue a second book and another series. It is often the case that success imposes a sequel; in some instances—and I think of cinema in particular—the sequel is then followed by another sequel and that by another and so on. I am conscious of the commercial aspect of success, that desire to squeeze as much juice as possible out of a good idea, so it was with a mixture of apprehension and measured optimism that I set about writing *Gondola on the Murray: A Feast by the River*.

I do not say this under the spell of false modesty; I have already talked about the difficulty of writing meaningful cookery books when almost anything that there is to know has already been published! All I can contribute is a repackaging of the basic rules of Italian cooking in a manner that I think is relevant to Australian conditions. I also restate, among other things, the belief that unless we prepare more food at home, for family and friends, taking advantage of what is readily available in Australia at a reasonable price, we will be further colonised by the café society and the takeaway shops owned by international corporations.

What thrilled me more than anything else about the *Gondola* experience was public reaction. I think people were pleased to see their own country reflected on screen through the combination of food, characters and location. British authors of cookery books who are also television chefs nearly always top the Australian book sale charts, particularly if these chefs happen to be fat or pretty. *Gondola* perhaps did not reach vertiginous heights, but I know that it touched many people deeply and, I hope, in a way that will last in time. It's success also confirms for me that if we had more money made available to the ABC there would be more homemade shows of great quality and integrity.

I am also pleased that my work highlights a piece of regional Australia. More often than not, food and entertainment are associated with the city, where the real action is perceived to be. Rural Australia is not very trendy, while the other side of the Great Divide counts for even less. I hope I have suggested to viewers and readers that there is a reality that is both dynamic and culturally rich outside the major metropolitan centres. These points weren't lost on many people I have spoken to since the series, which I find satisfying. Many were touched by the Murray River, not only by its intrinsic beauty, but by what it has come to represent in contemporary Australia—a source of life.

If the barriers between city and country were reduced a little, we could see more professional people—at least those starting off at the lower level—moving to the bush. With the great emphasis that state tourism organisations now place on regional and remote Australia, the pressure is on the bush to provide better services in the hospitality industry. That goal will never be achieved at the current pace, because professionals think there is no money in the bush, and that it is a dead place anyway. So many of them (and I am not talking about the real high-fliers) remain in the city, stuck in a rat race, instead of taking advantage of the great opportunities that exist in the bush.

But back to the food. Food should be the business of hope, passion and celebration. The food in this book, like *Gondola*, comes from a gutsy Australian region, known for its vastness, dryness and meanness. When the wind picks up speed, the paddocks go flying into the sky! So this book testifies to the resilient Australian character. More than that, it is a genuine attempt to feature food that family, friends and community can eat together, and together forge a strong sense of place with a strong sense of purpose.

I am delighted to include the voice of Loretta Sartori, a well-kept Victorian secret, in this book. Loretta is truly a master in the art of pastry and desserts, much admired and respected by many people in the food industry, particularly in Victoria, who have had the pleasure

INTRODUCTION

and privilege of sharing her knowledge. Like me, Loretta's ancestors came from the Veneto region of Italy. When I invited her to collaborate with me, I was looking for an experienced hand who could reinterpret some of the great Italian desserts and make them accessible to Australian readers. This book would not have been the same without her. Often desserts are stuck at the end of Italian cookery books like afterthoughts. More often they are uninspiring and deritvative. Loretta has presented a thoughtful, inspired and accurate range of sweets; a compendium of what you can make that is both possible and authentic. What an honour to have found someone with a superlative mastery of her art, a distinctive Italian accent, and a little bit of a gondola in her heart!

OASIS CITY

Rose-red city in the angles of a cut up
green anthology: grape stanzas, citrus strophes,
I like your dirt cliffs and chimney-broom palm trees,

your pipe dream under dust, in its head of pressure,
I enjoy your landscape blown from the Pleistocene
and reefed in stick forests of tarmacadam blue.

Your river waltzed round thousands of loops to you
and never guessed. Now it's locked in a Grand Canal,
aerated with paddlewheels, feeder of kicking sprays,

its willows placid as geese outspread over young
or banner-streamed under flood. Hey, rose-red city
of the tragic fountain, of the expensive brink,

of crescent clubs, of flags basil white-and-tomato,
I love how you were invented and turned on:
the city as equipment, unpacking its intersections.

City dreamed wrongly true in Puglia and Antakya
with your unemployed orange-trunks globalised out of the ground,
I delight in the mountains your flat scrub calls to mind

and how you'd stack up if decanted over steep relief.
I praise your camel-train skies and tanglefoot red-gums
and how you mine water, speed it up to chrome lace and slow it

to culture's ingredients. How you learn your tolerance
on hideous pans far out, by the crystals of land sweat.
Along high-speed vistas, action breaks out of you,

but sweeter are its arrivals back inside
dust-walls of evergreen, air watered with raisins and weddings,
the beer of days pickers, the crash wine of night pickers.

LES MURRAY

ANTIPASTI

I read a comment on antipasto by a food reviewer that left me somewhat perplexed. He said that whatever he was eating at a particular establishment as a form of appetiser — which is the role of antipasto — put the traditional 'open platter' to shame. I agree — many antipasto platters are either so boring or so over-the-top that they simply look disgusting.

First of all, less is more. An antipasto should never be so large and generous as to replace the proper meal. It should always be small and tasty and tastefully presented. The days of a frittata with asparagus, oysters, roasted capsicums, prawns, salame and mortadella and olives on a base of large lettuce leaves are blessedly over. One, two or three elements is all that is needed, especially when the typical Italian ingredients that would make an antipasto really special are not existent here in Australia.

While it is true that Australia boasts a fabulous array of fresh and clean foods, in many departments we are really lacking. This is no more apparent than in antipasto. For instance, a few perfect slices of mortadella, properly sliced — thinly, that is — are unbeatable with delicate warm, white bread. The problem is that in Australia you can dream about mortadella, but you just cannot get the real thing. Gigantic mortadella with peppercorns and pistachios, pink and delicate and soft and flavoursome, are only in my dreams. Smaller ones, with chunky pieces of meat, flavoured or otherwise, I can only eat in Italy, and not everywhere there either.

What about prosciutto? Once again, this pillar of the antipasto selection is but a pale imitation in the Antipodes. Too salty, too wet, too unripened, too home-made, too dry; in short, inconsistent. And prosciutto with rockmelon? Well, you'd have to have a lot of courage to propose this dish, mostly because neither ingredient stands up to scrutiny. Salame is much in the same category. People have tried, some got near the mark, some efforts are very good, but we are not there yet.

Cured meats take a long time to prepare, the variables are many and the costs high. Few people are prepared to undertake any of these preparations at home, even if they have experience in preserving meats.

It is therefore somewhat easier and wiser to serve French-style charcuterie as antipasto — rillettes, terrines and pâtés. With the constituent elements cooked for hours and blended with fat, they are attractive to look at, modern in approach and traditional in technique. But in truth, most of these are too challenging for home cooks, and many just do not have the time.

So, where does this leave our antipasto platter? Somewhat in limbo, I fear. Luckily, in Australia, we are a little more free to experiment with the notion of antipasto. Many new dishes that fit into that category are being invented all the time. Many are Mediterranean-inspired, making Australia more multicultural a cuisine than any Mediterranean country. The addition of Asian elements is also making the Australian antipasto even more exotic and variable.

Antipasto has two choices: stay in limbo or renew itself. While I still present classic antipasto morsels, I know that by using all the influences available to us in Australia, minimally and in good taste, the future will change.

IL PANE

BREAD

*This is a soft bread, ideal as an accompaniment to delicate foods like poached salmon,
light terrines or cured meats and, with the addition of dried fruit, cheese. The bread is better
suited when made as small rolls or baguettes. Toasted slices from the baguettes are delicious
as an elegant breakfast or a creative bruschetta at lunchtime.*

Makes about 25 small rolls

PREPARATION TIME: 1 HOUR 30 MINUTES

COOKING TIME: 10 MINUTES

500 g (1 lb) plain (all-purpose) flour
1½ teaspoons dried yeast
50 g (1½ oz) lard or butter
a pinch of salt
a pinch of sugar
enough warm water to obtain a soft dough

Mix the flour, yeast, butter, salt and sugar together on the bench or in a bowl and gradually add warm water. Place the dough in a bowl, cover with a tea-towel and let it rise for about 1 hour. (Perhaps it is best to place the lot inside a plastic bag to avoid contact with the air.)

Flour a workbench and stretch the dough by pressing it with the fingertips to a thickness of 2.5 cm (1 inch). Cut out rolls with a round or oval disc. If preparing baguettes, take a piece of dough and pull it out with your fingers. Avoid using a rolling pin as the pressure interferes with the dough. Cover and allow the rolls to rise in a warm place.

Preheat the oven to 200°C (400°F). Transfer the rolls or baguettes to a baking tray and cook for 10 minutes or until golden. Baguettes may take a little longer.

To MAKE FOCACCIA, replace 30 g (1 oz) fat from the recipe with 30 ml (1 fl oz) olive oil. Stretch it with your hands and place over it any dried herbs such as sage or rosemary. After the second rising stick your thumb into the dough to create a rough surface all over. Sprinkle with water, a little oil and rock salt. Bake in an oven preheated to 200°C (400°F) until golden.

VARIATIONS
It is possible to substitute one-third of the plain flour with polenta, farrum, besan (chickpea flour) or buckwheat, and adding either seeds or herbs.

When preparing bread for cheese, add 100 g (3½ oz) sultanas softened in a little water or chopped walnuts or dried figs.

PIADINA CON PANCETTA E CAPPUCCIO
FLAT BREAD WITH PANCETTA AND CABBAGE

Piadina is a form of flat bread without yeast cooked on a hot plate, much like some Indian bread. It is found generally in the Romagna region of Italy, especially around the coastal towns of Rimini and Ravenna. It is the only part of Italy, to my knowledge, where this bread is made.

I would really like to think that piadina is related to pita bread and other similar eastern breads. This theory is supported by the fact that the Byzantines, the Greeks of the eastern Roman Empire, ruled around Ravenna for quite some time in the first millennium. Fancy theory, but why not!

In that part of Italy you will find piadinerie: *shops where they roll out a piadina in front of you, cook it there and then, and fill it with your choice of stuffing — stracchino cheese, thinly sliced prosciutto, rocket and parmesan and so on. Sounds like Italian souvlaki, does it not?*

In my restaurant I often serve piadina as a starter, filled with shredded duck cooked in a Chinese fashion. Once again, this is another fun dish, one that you can teach children, who can use it as a pizza base, among other things.

Stracchino cheese and prosciutto are ideal as a stuffing, as are salami and other cured meats. My preference is for braised cabbage with shreds of cooked pancetta.

Serves 6

PREPARATION TIME: 1 HOUR ALL UP

PIADINA

warm water

up to 300 g (10 oz) butter or, for a
better result, dripping

500 g (1 lb) plain (all-purpose) flour

a pinch of bicarbonate of soda (baking soda)

a pinch of salt

water

FILLING

1 red onion, chopped

2 tablespoons olive oil

butter

1 Savoy cabbage, thinly sliced

250 mL (1 cup) milk

salt and pepper

6 slices pancetta, thinly sliced

2 tablespoons olive oil, extra

To make the piadina, fill a bowl with warm water. Place butter or dripping in another bowl and place it inside the bowl with warm water to soften the fat.

Make a crater in the flour and add the bicarbonate of soda and salt. Gradually pour in the melted fat and some water to make a dough. Keep mixing, adding water as you go, until you obtain a fairly firm dough.

Break off enough dough to roll out a circle of 15 cm (6 inches) in diameter and 4 mm (¼ inch) thick. Cook it without any oil on a hot iron pan or any other flat metal surface set over a high flame. Turn frequently and prick the base with a fork to stop it from rising and forming big bubbles. The pastry will 'set' and dry out as it cooks. If you keep the dough thicker (say, 8 mm or ⅓ inch), you can split it in half through the middle, although I don't think it is necessary. Repeat with the rest of the dough.

To make the filling, fry the onion in oil and butter. Add the cabbage and when this is wilted, add the milk. Season with salt and pepper. Keep cooking until the cabbage is almost a jam. If it dries out during cooking, add a little more milk or some stock or water.

In another frying pan, lightly sauté the pancetta in the olive oil.

Place the cabbage and some pancetta on the piadina, fold over and enjoy with a glass of light red.

CROSTINI DI FEGATINI, ACCIUGHE E CAPPERI

CROSTINI OF LIVER, ANCHOVIES AND CAPERS

Crostini are toasted slices of crusty bread. Mostly small crostini are used as finger food, but in today's changing style of eating they can be included under the rubric of antipasto. Either way, crostini are delicious if the topping is interesting. Here I suggest a use for chicken livers mixed with some anchovies (for salt) and capers (for acidity). If you happen to have livers from ducks or game birds, all the better.

Makes 6 large crostini

PREPARATION TIME: 30 MINUTES

COOKING TIME: 10 MINUTES

300 g (10 oz) chicken livers
2 bay leaves
4 sage leaves
olive oil
6 good-quality anchovies
60 mL (¼ cup) white wine
2 tablespoons capers
salt and pepper
6 slices grilled or toasted crusty bread

In a skillet toss the livers, bay and sage leaves with some olive oil until the livers change colour. Add the anchovies, break them down with a wooden spoon, and add the wine to lift the juices from the bottom of the pan.

Add the capers, pepper and any necessary salt. Do not overcook or the livers will be leathery. Mash the livers coarsely and spread over the bread. You may, if you wish, rub some oil on the bread before putting on the liver.

LE POLPETTE DELLE ZIE

AUNTIE'S BREAD PATTIES

Auntie Cathy and Auntie Maria were made famous in the first series of Gondola on the
Murray *for their ability to make the best ferricelli pasta with immense deftness and speed.
I have not attempted to explain ferricelli in the pasta section because they are too tricky. But the
zie are also famous, at least in their own families — and zia Cathy has five children, plus two
of mine, who seem to be at her house around dinner time quite frequently — for the
most exquisite polpette made of bread and cheese.*

Serves 4

PREPARATION TIME: 30 MINUTES

COOKING TIME: 40 MINUTES

2 packed cups slightly stale, Italian-style
bread, crust removed

1 cup grated cheese, eg Parmesan

2 eggs

2 tablespoons finely shredded fresh parsley

salt and pepper

water

olive oil

3 cups tomato sauce (see page 37)

1 cup peas

Place the bread in a food processor and crumb it. Add
the cheese, eggs, parsley and seasoning. Blend until it
turns into a firm dough-like mixture. It may need a
little water to come together.

With your hands, make oval-shaped patties from
the mixture. Seal them with a little olive oil, a few
at a time.

Heat the tomato sauce, add the peas and cook for
15 minutes.

Add the bread *polpette* and cook for at least 30
minutes. Add water if the sauce becomes too dry.

The result should be stew-like, with bread *polpette*
and peas.

BAKING BLIND

The act of baking blind ensures that the pastry crust will be thoroughly cooked, resulting in a crisp dough, rather than a sluggish opaque pastry shell that will not digest well, let alone eat well.

The procedure is simple enough. Roll out the pastry to line the tin, then refrigerate for about 1 hour.

Preheat the oven to 180°C (350°F). Line the pastry with foil or non-stick baking paper, ensuring that the lining covers the base and comes up the sides beyond the walls. Fill the pastry shell with baking weights — some folks use dried beans or metal pellets, but I prefer rice, which is cheap and effective. When you fill the cavity, ensure that the weights support the walls of the tart. I find it best to attend to this and leave fewer weights in the centre. The weights will support the walls as the pastry bakes and keep the base flat.

Baking can take up to 30 minutes, longer if the cavity is deeper. Check that the pastry case is thoroughly cooked. If you notice an opaque greyish area it will require further baking. If so, remove the bulk of the weights and return the shell to the oven.

Once this base is cooked, you can add the filling. The pastry will not burn with the additional cooking time for the filling; in fact the filling insulates and prevents the base/sides from burning. The only exception to this rule is if the oven is set on a higher than suggested temperature. **LS**

TORTINO DI ZUCCHINI

SAVOURY ZUCCHINI TART

The word 'tortino' in Italian has many meanings. For me it is simply a savoury tart, sometimes with a lid and sometimes, as in these recipes, uncovered.

*Like sformato, the tortino is versatile and elegant, and suitable for many occasions —
a lunch, a picnic or a serious dinner party.*

Tortinos, however, rely on a pastry that is quite short, crunchy and ethereal at the same time. It is worth bothering with the mastery of this pastry as it gives brilliant results for both savoury and sweet dishes. There is something 'aristocratic' about this pastry, which belongs to the fine cooking tradition.

Makes 1 × 23 cm (9 inch) tortino

PREPARATION TIME: I HOUR

COOKING TIME: 35 MINUTES

PASTRY

185 g (6 oz) plain (all-purpose) flour

100 g (3½ oz) unsalted butter, chilled and finely diced

1 tablespoon milk

1 egg

a pinch of castor (superfine) sugar

a pinch of salt

FILLING

500 g (1 lb) zucchini, thinly sliced

extra-virgin olive oil

1 clove garlic, crushed

1 small sprig rosemary

2 egg yolks

30 g (1 oz) grana cheese, grated

125 mL (½ cup) cream

salt and pepper

grated nutmeg (only if freshly grated)

To make the pastry, in an electric mixer (or by hand), blend the flour and butter together and, with the mixer going on a low speed, pour in the milk and egg. Mix until just combined. Do not overmix. The dough can be rolled out immediately and used to line the tart case. Rest and chill for 2 hours before baking. If not rolling out until later, wrap the dough in cling wrap and refrigerate.

To make the filling, fry the zucchini gently in a small amount of oil with the garlic and rosemary. Cook until dry and the juices have evaporated. Remove from the heat, and discard the rosemary and garlic.

In a bowl, add the rest of the ingredients to the zucchini and mix.

Preheat the oven to 180°C (350°F).

Roll out the pastry to line a 23 cm (9 inch) tart. Chill for 1 hour. Bake 'blind' in the oven (see Loretta's comments on page 22). Cool when ready.

Lower the oven temperature to 160°C (325°F).

Pour in the zucchini mixture and bake until set, about 35 minutes. The mixture should set firm, and not have a wobble about it at all.

OLIVE OIL

My passion for olive oil is stronger than ever. In the last four years I have had the privilege of making oil with my friend Gianni Grigoletto from olives entirely harvested in one specific district of Australia, the Sunraysia region.

We have come to the conclusion that, for ourselves, mono-varietal oil is the way to go — at least for the time being — because you can detect specific flavours by variety, geographical position and degree of olive maturation. While the development of the oil industry in Australia is still in its infancy, it is important to know what material we are dealing with, and to identify particular trees and flavours. This is even more important if we value cottage products, in line with the thinking of the organic food movement. Even within the same region, mono-varietals are so very different because of different soil conditions that they never cease to amaze and excite me.

We also believe that we should try to exploit the local genetic patrimony. Where the trees are giving good results, with distinct Australian accents, why go looking for something imported that has yet to prove itself? Large commercial concerns may have another view, and that's fine for commercial operators who wish to take risks in the hope of greater returns. From the point of view of sound practices and our own gastronomy, locality should come first, if the genetic material is sound.

Dr Antonio Cimato, an expert on olives at the Italian National Research Centre is quoted in Dr Michael Burr's seminal work on Australian olives, saying that we should be looking for unique olives in Australia, rather than holding out for imports of varieties famous in their own environments.

Much of this 'sorting out' work should have been undertaken many years ago by really aggressive government bodies determined to implement import replacement programs. Much research was carried out by enthusiasts like Dr Burr and Dr Grigoletto, most often without reward.

Bureaucrats and other government operators did not foresee the growth of the olive oil market: one of them, a friend who was running the minister's office in a well-known Victorian government department that gave money away like confetti to all manners of failed ventures, told me dismissively that olive oil was going to go with the integration of ethnic communities into the mainstream. Can you believe that?

What I do not like and do not encourage people to buy is thin, generic olive oil or even extra virgins that look like they have had the life squeezed out of them. Many supermarkets settle for these oils, which, while correct and even faultless, are boring in the extreme. A friend I love was making gorgeous sourdough bread for his family on a daily basis and drizzling it with a terribly nondescript oil, one of which was mildly rancid. I pointed out to him that going to the trouble of making beautiful bread to ruin it with ordinary oil was defeating the purpose.

There are many other oils that are perfectly legitimate for a variety of uses. I am not against them at all. I sometimes use olive oil out of laziness, for sometimes it may even be better to dress a salad with something else!

OLIVE OIL PASTRY

In A Gondola on the Murray, *I gave a recipe for tortino with weeds. People were amazed that I would cook with weeds, including stinging nettles. To my mind, nettles are very good, as good as spinach, especially when picked young and tender. That tortino used a very traditional lard pastry, which is as charming as it is rustic.*

Another fabulous pastry, much used in Italian cooking, replaces the lard or butter with olive oil. It is suitable for fillings that have a stronger flavour such as broccoli, pancetta or sun-dried tomatoes. The oil helps to accentuate strong flavours, while butter is more suitable for subtle flavours such as asparagus.

As Loretta puts it, 'It is not unusual to find oil replacing butter in Italian pastry recipes. Butter is not a typical fat used in all regions — it is represented more in the north than the south. Oil will impart a crispness and distinctive flavour and texture. Oil-based doughs are easier to work with as they are elastic, rather than "short".'

PREPARATION TIME: 15 MINUTES

100 mL (3½ fl oz) water
125 mL (½ cup) olive oil
300 g (10 oz) plain (all-purpose) flour
a pinch of salt

To make the pastry, combine the water and oil and pour into the flour and salt. Slowly mix until you get a dough. Do not overwork. Refrigerate for 2 hours before using. Roll out and bake blind according to the instructions on page 22 before fillling.

TORTINO DI BROCCOLI E PANCETTA

TART OF BROCCOLI AND PANCETTA

Here is a terrific tart that combines the oil pastry with two gutsy ingredients, broccoli and pancetta.

*Rest the pastry to prevent shrinkage before using. Oil pastry has an elastic nature once it has been formed and lightly kneaded, hence the two-hour resting period. Upon extending the dough — by rolling it out to line the tart — you may notice some 'pulling back'. Ease the pastry into position, press the dough onto the walls and allow to overlap slightly. Chill as you prepare the filling, and trim off the excess dough before you add the filling. **LS***

Serves up to 8

PREPARATION TIME: 20 MINUTES

COOKING TIME: 45 MINUTES

1 recipe Olive Oil Pastry (see page 26)
400 g (14 oz) broccoli, cut into small pieces
½ cup thinly sliced and chopped pancetta
2 egg yolks
125 mL (½ cup) cream
50 g (1½ oz) grated grana or pecorino
salt and pepper

Prepare the pastry according to the instructions on page 26 and let it rest.

In the meantime, blanch the broccoli in plenty of salted boiling water to soften a little. Plunge into cold water to stop the cooking and to prevent loss of colour. Chop them a little more if needed. Combine with all the other ingredients.

Roll out the pastry to line a 23 cm (9 inch) tin. Let it rest again in the refrigerator for 2 hours.

Preheat the oven to 180°C (350°F).

Blind bake the pastry following the instructions on page 22.

Pour the broccoli mixture into the prepared pastry shell and cook in the oven for 20–25 minutes. The mixture sets fairly quickly, so keep an eye on it.

FRITTO MISTO DI VERDURE ALL'ITALIANA

FRIED VEGETABLES IN BATTER

*Here the Italians compete with the Japanese for crunchy deep-fried vegetables in batter.
There are many recipes for batter, but the one I like the most is very much like
a tempura. The water has to be very chilled.*

PREPARATION TIME: 15 MINUTES

COOKING TIME: 3 MINUTES

1 cup plain flour
250 mL (1 cup) chilled water
a selection of vegetables of your choice
oil for frying

Combine the flour and water in a bowl.

Prepare the vegetables, cutting them into even-sized shapes and pieces.

Heat the oil in a pan. Dip the vegetables in the batter, then place in the oil. (Do this in batches so you don't lower the temperature of the oil too much.) As soon as the vegetables turn a golden colour, sprinkle them with a few drops of chilled water. (Be careful, the splatter can be dangerous if you overdo it and you may even cause a fire if you really overdo it.) I do not know why, but the cold water — a few droplets — on and around whatever you are frying will ensure their crunchiness.

Drain well on kitchen paper.

*Clockwise from top: Strudel di Verdure (page 32),
Fritto Misto di Verdure all'Italiana: broccoli e peperoni (page 29),
Fiori di Zucchini (page 30), Sformato di Peperoni (page 40)*

FIORI DI ZUCCHINI

DEEP-FRIED ZUCCHINI FLOWERS

Many types of flowers can be eaten, but to me, deep-fried zucchini flowers are the best. Use the same batter as for Fried Vegetables (see page 29). The flowers can be filled, and the easiest filling is one of ricotta and grana cheese. As you become more experienced you can fill them with bocconcini and anchovies or ricotta and ham and so on.

Serves 4

PREPARATION TIME: 30 MINUTES
COOKING TIME: 5 MINUTES

BATTER
250 g (8 oz) plain (all-purpose) flour
a pinch of salt
250 mL (1 cup) warm water
4 egg whites

FILLING
200 g (7 oz) ricotta
50 g (1½ oz) grana cheese, grated
2 egg yolks
salt and pepper
12 zucchini flowers
olive or vegetable oil

To make the batter, combine the flour, salt and water. Just before using, beat the egg whites to firm peaks. Fold into the flour mixture.

Mix together the cheeses, eggs and seasoning. Carefully spoon into the flowers, taking care not to overfill.

Heat some olive or vegetable oil in a pan until hot. (A small domestic deep-fryer is ideal, but it can all be done perfectly by frying in a shallow pan with an inch of oil.) Plunge the flowers into the batter and fry in the oil.

Drain well on kitchen paper.

CASSONI FRITTI

DEEP-FRIED PASTRIES

*There isn't much to these more-ish morsels, except that you never see them anywhere.
They are made with the same egg dough that is used for pasta, which is then filled and
deep-fried. Folded discs of dough will give a half-moon shape. Sometimes these fried pastries
are known as panzarotti. The filling has to be something that 'holds' during the immersion
in hot oil. Cheese mixed with vegetables or meat like salami or prosciutto will do that.*

Makes 40–50 cassoni/panzarotti

PREPARATION TIME: 1 HOUR

COOKING TIME: 5 MINUTES

PASTA

500 g (1 lb) plain (all-purpose) flour

5 eggs or more, depending on their size

1 tablespoon olive oil

FILLING

100 g (3½ oz) prosciutto

300 g (10 oz) ricotta

100 g (3½ oz) pecorino
or grana cheese, grated

olive oil

To make the pasta, mix the ingredients together gradually until a smooth paste is obtained. Wrap in cling wrap and rest for at least 2 hours in the refrigerator. (This prevents a brittle pastry.)

To make the filling, place the prosciutto in the food processor and render it to a paste. Add the other ingredients (make sure the ricotta is perfectly dry). This is a basic filling — use whatever you like.

Roll the pasta through a pasta machine until you reach the finest setting. You can cut out discs with a glass (and lose some dough). Wet the edges with water or egg and fold over. Or place the filling at 3 cm (1¼ inch) distances on the bottom part of the sheet facing you, fold over, and with a cutter or a glass, cut between the fillings (rounded side away from the fold) to obtain perfect cassoni. Seal the edges, applying pressure with a fork. The pastries can be made ahead to this point and refrigerated until you are ready to fry.

Deep-fry in olive oil, drain on kitchen paper and serve at once.

STRUDEL DI VERDURE
VEGETABLE STRUDEL

I have always been fascinated by the art of making strudel and the theatrics of stretching a thin dough by hand. My sisters would undertake this task on important occasions and I remember the ritual of stretching a huge sheet of pastry over a white linen cloth. If you work with just a small amount of dough, the task is not so daunting and after a little practice, you get the hang of it.

It is possible to fill this strudel with a range of fillings. A simple one is spinach and ricotta, or asparagus and a small amount of ricotta. Or use roasted capsicum. If you wish, toss the cooked spinach in some butter and garlic to add extra flavour. If you do, combine all ingredients when cold.

Makes 2 strudel

PREPARATION TIME: 1 HOUR
COOKING TIME: 30 MINUTES

PASTRY
250 g (8 oz) plain (all-purpose) flour
200 mL (7 fl oz) warm water
1 tablespoon oil or melted butter
1 teaspoon sugar
1 teaspoon vinegar
a pinch of salt

FILLING
3 cups ricotta
3 cups cooked spinach, chopped
and all water squeezed out
1 cup grated parmesan
4 eggs
salt and pepper
melted butter

To make the pastry, tip the flour onto a bench and make a well in the middle. Gradually pour in the water and the rest of the ingredients, mixing them until the flour has been absorbed. (You may need more or less of the water, depending on the conditions and the flour you are using.) Work the pastry until it is elastic and smooth like the cheek of a baby. Grease it lightly with butter, wrap it in a piece of cloth and cover it with a metal bowl or pot that has been warmed up. (The slightly warmed environment makes the dough malleable.) Allow to rest for 20–30 minutes while you prepare the filling.

To make the filling, combine all the ingredients except the butter.

After 20–30 minutes split the pastry in half. Place one half on a floured cloth, roll it out as much as possible with a rolling pin and then stretch it gently using the knuckles of both hands from under the pastry and by pulling the sides until the pastry is transparent.

If you break this pastry you can patch it up with another piece of dough. Trim the edges because they are invariably a little thicker.

Preheat the oven to 180°C (350°F). Grease a baking tray.

Brush the pastry with butter and place the filling on the top part of the sheet away from you. Pick up the top end of the cloth and pull it towards yourself so that the strudel will roll on itself. Make sure the roll falls on the prepared baking dish. Tuck the end bits under so that the mixture will not escape and paint the surface with more melted butter. Repeat with the rest of the pastry and ingredients.

Cook for 30 minutes or a little more, depending on the filling. The surface of the pastry should be golden.

FRITTATA DI CIPOLLE E PATATE CON VECCHIO BALSAMICO

FRITTATA OF ONIONS AND POTATO WITH OLD BALSAMIC

Here is a classic — perhaps one done to death in trendy magazines — but the addition of aged balsamic vinegar makes this dish ideal for a special dinner party. The balsamic vinegar must be very old, and instead of being poured over the frittata is served in tiny amounts in small glasses and sipped with mouthfuls of frittata. In this case, not only do you have to forget wine, but it is compulsory to offer a clean and crisp glass of water. The interaction between the potato and onions in the frittata with the extra old balsamic is very special and is another taste sensation not to be missed.

Serves 4

PREPARATION TIME: 40 MINUTES

COOKING TIME: 15 MINUTES

olive oil

butter

2 medium-sized red onions, thinly sliced

3 medium-sized potatoes, partly steamed, sliced

8 free-range eggs

250 mL (1 cup) cream

½ cup grated parmesan

salt and pepper

aged balsamic vinegar

Preheat the oven to 180°C (350°F).

In a metal pan that can hold at least 2 cm (¾ inch) of egg mixture and that can go into the oven, heat a little oil and butter. Cook the onions until soft. Add the potatoes and cook them until they are soft and the flavours are well integrated.

In the meantime, break the eggs into a bowl and mix with the cream and cheese. When the onion and potato base is ready, add the egg mixture and, with a spatula, integrate the eggs with the rest of the pan ingredients except the vinegar.

Place the pan in the oven. When in the oven, keep your eye on it as you want the frittata simply to set, not cook hard; about 15 minutes. Metal pans often have a strange smell when heated, so ease out the frittata as soon as possible.

Serve warm, cut into slices, with tiny glasses of aged balsamico and glasses of water.

CIPOLLINE IN AGRO-DOLCE

This frittata is delicious, yet I can't allow the opportunity to pass without mention of one of my favourites: *cipolline in agro-dolce* (sweet and sour onions). Often when presenting an Italian-style buffet, these onions are overlooked in favour of artichokes, roasted stuffed capsicum or zucchini flowers. But once sampled, the onions are quickly depleted.

To make, toss whole baby onions or shallots in butter and a little brown sugar to caramelise. Once the colour is achieved, add a good splash of balsamic vinegar, then a handful of plump sultanas. Move the onions around in your pan and place a lid on top. Cook until tender, remove the lid and reduce the juices by increasing the heat, tossing occasionally. The dish is ready when the reduction is thick and glossy and the onions are tender. **LS**

CROCHETTE DI FONDO DI CARCIOFO

ARTICHOKE CROQUETTES

I cannot stress enough how unique and wonderful artichoke is. People keep telling me that they find the so-called 'choke' unappealing and I agree with them: the hairy choke should not be eaten, and artichokes with a developed choke are too old, if you ask me. That tends to happen late in the season, so inspect your artichokes before buying them.

But even when the carciofi are oldish, their fondo — the cup-like base — is delicious and a speciality in its own right. Make sure you buy artichokes at a very cheap price when you want these 'bottoms', like three or more for a dollar.

Crochettes are finger-shaped morsels that are deep-fried and served with a sauce.

Serves 6

PREPARATION TIME: 1 HOUR
COOKING TIME: 5 MINUTES

12 artichokes
lemon juice
125 mL (½ cup) olive oil
3 cloves garlic, chopped
½ cup chopped parsley
salt and pepper
250 mL (1 cup) Chicken Stock (see page 61)
½ cup grated parmesan
½ cup ricotta
2 eggs

TO FRY
plain (all-purpose) flour
extra eggs
breadcrumbs
olive oil

To obtain the 'bottom' of the artichokes, remove all the outer leaves and spoon out the core or choke. You will be left with a fleshy, cup-like base. Drop the prepared artichokes into water with some lemon juice to prevent discolouration.

Heat the oil in a small saucepan, add the garlic, artichokes and parsley. Add a little salt and pepper and then the stock. Cook until the artichokes are soft and the liquid has reduced.

Mash the 'bases' in their juice, cool, then add the cheeses and eggs to obtain a firm mixture. Spread the paste out to 1 cm (½ inch) thickness. Cut away small finger-like shapes, roll them in flour, egg and breadcrumbs.

Heat some oil in a frying pan and deep-fry the fingers in batches. Serve hot with a homemade tomato sauce (see following page).

SUGO DI POMODORO

TOMATO SAUCE

Makes 250 mL (1 cup)

PREPARATION AND COOKING TIME: 35 MINUTES

4 tablespoons olive oil
2 cloves garlic, whole
1 × 400 g (14 oz) can tomatoes

Heat the oil in a skillet and fry the garlic until fragrant. Remove and discard the garlic. Crush the tomatoes with a fork and add to the pan, and cook for 20 minutes over a low–medium heat.

PEPERONI ARROSTITI CON RIPIENO DI ACCIUGHE E CAPPERI

ROASTED CAPSICUM STUFFED WITH ANCHOVIES AND CAPERS

A very appetising starter. Capsicum make excellent containers for a pesto of anchovies, garlic, capers and parsley with a very good olive oil. The success of this dish depends on the quality of the anchovies, the capers and the olive oil especially.

Serves 6

PREPARATION TIME: 45 MINUTES

COOKING TIME: 30 MINUTES

3 red or yellow capsicum (bell peppers)

12 anchovy fillets

2 cloves garlic

1 tablespoon small capers

3 tablespoons chopped parsley

extra-virgin olive oil

Preheat the oven to 180°C (350°F) and roast the capsicum until the skins blister. Allow to cool a little, peel the skins, and split each capsicum into 2–3 lobes. Discard the seeds and membranes.

Place the rest of the ingredients in a food processor and gradually add the olive oil until a wet paste is formed.

Place a spoonful of paste on each piece of capsicum, douse with extra oil and eat with crusty bread.

SFORMATO DI PEPERONI
SFORMATO OF CAPSICUM

Sformati are cooked in moulds like custards and, like custards, they contain eggs.
They rely on the béchamel sauce for setting and are cooked in a water bath.
In a way, they combine a smart way of cooking with the
elements of old gastronomy.

Serves 6

PREPARATION TIME: 1 HOUR
COOKING TIME: 35 MINUTES

5 red capsicum (bell peppers)
250 mL (1 cup) Béchamel Sauce (see page 45), firm, not too liquid
3 eggs
½ cup grated parmesan
salt and pepper

Preheat the oven to 180°C (350°F).

Roast the capsicum in the oven until the skins blister, about 30 minutes. Remove from the oven, cool, then peel, discarding the seeds and skins. Purée the flesh in a food processor.

Lower the oven to 140°C (275°F).

Combine the capsicum purée with all the other ingredients. Mix well and place in 6 disposable plastic moulds (available from supermarkets) or ceramic soufflé ramekins. Place the ramekins in a baking tray, pour warm water to come halfway up the sides and bake in the oven until set, about 35 minutes. The mixture should set firm and not have a wobble to it at all.

THE GREAT CAPSICUM DISASTER

You must be very careful when using capsicum. There seem to be times when their water content is so high that it is virtually impossible to cook them to the point where they set. I wanted to highlight the *sformato* at a dinner in Melbourne during the Melbourne Food Festival. A long table of some 70 people — including well-known and scary food writers as well as assorted foodies — were assembled in the warehouse at the Vital Ingredient in Clarendon Street, South Melbourne. As I live and work in the bush, it was easy selling me to a large crowd of curious people who would otherwise have to travel a long distance just to check me out.

The bluff worked well, and the dinner was oversubscribed. The *sformato*, however, would not set, not even after a second attempt. Too much water in the purée — and lack of experience in dealing with the problem — resulted in a non-setting glug that I proceeded to spoon as a quenelle rather that as a proud, free-standing moulded shape. Ah, the humiliation was such that I burst into tears and made an utter fool of myself in front of other people! The experience was to repeat itself with some other recipe in another place less than a year down the track. Another humiliation I cannot bear to recount! **SdP**

SFORMATO DI ZUCCHINI
SFORMATO OF ZUCCHINI

*You can play on variations by adding a couple of tablespoons
of goat curd to the zucchini mixture.*

Serves 6

PREPARATION TIME: 1 HOUR
COOKING TIME: 35 MINUTES

5 medium-sized zucchini, grated

2 tablespoons butter

250 mL (1 cup) Béchamel Sauce
(see page 45), firm, not too liquid

3 eggs

½ cup grated parmesan

salt and pepper

a pinch of freshly grated nutmeg
(omit if not fresh)

Sauté the zucchini in butter until cooked. Place in a colander and allow to stand for a while to drain off the excess juice. Purée in food processor (a couple of turns will do).

Preheat the oven to 160°C (325°F).

Combine the zucchini purée with all the other ingredients. Mix well and place in 6 disposable plastic moulds (available from supermarkets) or ceramic soufflé ramekins. Place the ramekins in a baking tray, pour warm water to come halfway up the sides and bake in the oven until set, about 35 minutes. The mixture should set firm and not have a wobble to it at all.

SFORMATO DI PATATE E PARMIGIANO

SFORMATO OF POTATO AND PARMESAN

This sformato is an excellent vegetarian starter, but I suggest that it be used more as a vegetable accompaniment to a substantial winter dish, such a rib roast or any other 'big' meat dish.

Serves 6

PREPARATION TIME: 1 HOUR

COOKING TIME: 35 MINUTES

5 medium-sized potatoes

250 mL (1 cup) Béchamel Sauce (see page 45), firm, not too liquid

1 cup coarsely chopped quality parmesan or grana cheese

salt and pepper

3 eggs

5 drops truffle oil

Preheat the oven to 160°C (325°F).

Roast or steam the potatoes. Peel and mash them with a fork, and combine with all the other ingredients. Mix well and place in 6 disposable plastic moulds (available from supermarkets) or ceramic soufflé ramekins. Place the ramekins in a baking tray, pour warm water to come halfway up the sides and bake in the oven until set, about 35 minutes. The mixture should set firm and not have a wobble to it at all.

SFORMATO DI FUNGHI PORCINI

SFORMATO OF PORCINI MUSHROOMS

Once again, a great starter with a drizzle of olive oil and shavings of parmesan next to a rocket salad or an accompaniment for winter dishes wherever mushrooms are appropriate.

Porcini mushrooms have a strong flavour. I find that diners unaccustomed to their 'in your face' aroma often return risotto con porcini as they say they cannot take it. Porcini are also expensive. In the sformato you can carefully 'regulate' their flavour to be strong or mild according to your preference. Just vary the amount and see where it takes you.

Serves 6

PREPARATION TIME: 30 MINUTES

COOKING TIME: 35 MINUTES

100 g (3½ oz) dried porcini
1 cup cultivated mushrooms
butter and olive oil
250 mL (1 cup) Béchamel Sauce
(see page 45), firm, not too liquid
1 egg
½ cup grated parmesan
salt and pepper

Reconstitute the porcini in a small bowl of hot water. Squeeze them dry and sauté them with the other mushrooms in a little butter and oil. Cook them until any liquid has reduced, then purée in a food processor.

Preheat the oven to 160°C (325°F).

Combine the mushrooms with all the other ingredients. Mix well and place in 6 disposable plastic moulds (available from supermarkets) or ceramic soufflé ramekins. Place the ramekins in a baking tray, pour warm water to come halfway up the sides and bake in the oven until set, about 35 minutes. The mixture should set firm and not have a wobble to it at all.

SALSA BESCIAMELLA

BÉCHAMEL SAUCE

*Béchamel is very important in the making of lasagna and sformati. It can also be
introduced into a rich meat sauce to give it a creamy, velvety texture.*

*This recipe should yield a fairly soft sauce. If it is too thick add more milk, or water.
If you think you have some lumps in it there is no reason to get depressed. Pass it through
a fine sieve and everything will be all right.*

Makes 2 L (8 cups)

PREPARATION TIME: 30 MINUTES

150 g (5 oz) unsalted butter
100 g (3½ oz) plain (all-purpose) flour
1.5 L (6 cups) hot milk
freshly grated nutmeg (optional)

Melt the butter and mix with the flour. Cook a little but without browning. Allow to cool and stir in the milk, bit by bit, mixing with a wooden spoon. Initially the mixture will be like a gluggy lump but as you add the milk it will break down more and more. Cook it gently for 20 minutes or more, taking care that it does not stick to the bottom of the pan. Add nutmeg to taste. Do not worry about flavouring the béchamel with onions — it will be incorporated with very strongly flavoured foods.

When using for *sformati*, the béchamel needs to be of a firm consistency, and the nutmeg should be omitted.

CARNE TRITATA AL PREZZEMOLO E LIMONE

RAW MINCE WITH PARSLEY AND LEMON

A lean eye fillet or another lean premium meat is preferable for this classic Piedmontese dish. I find it very filling, so a small amount will do as part of an antipasto or as the antipasto, especially if you can get hold of a few slices of white truffle! Truffles do come to Australia occasionally around October or November and they are stupidly expensive. But once, only once in a lifetime, food lovers should try to taste them, if only a few grams. Truffle oils and pastes are barely acceptable imitations of the real thing, but are useful aids as they introduce another dimension of flavour if used very sparingly and with compatible foods.

Serves 4

PREPARATION TIME: 15 MINUTES

300 g (10 oz) lean meat, minced
olive oil
salt and pepper
2 tablespoons chopped flat-leaf parsley
juice of ½ lemon

Mix all the ingredients but reserve the lemon juice for the last minute as it tends to discolour and 'cook' the meat. (It is possible to omit the lemon juice altogether.)

In many ways, this dish is eaten for its textural pleasure rather than a specific flavour.

QUAGLIE MARINATE ALLA GRIGLIA
GRILLED MARINATED QUAIL

I am so often reminded by my customers of how much they like quail, and yet these little succulent birds are not commonly available. They should be, not only because they are remarkably easy to cook, but they are cheap, dirt cheap — if you ask me.

Split them in half and keep the bones in. In the restaurants we take the bones out because that's part of our job, to make the diner eat comfortably. At home, use your hands and suck those little bones to the last tiny bit of flavour.

Serves 6 as a main

PREPARATION TIME: 15 MINUTES
COOKING TIME: 10 MINUTES

6 quail, cut along the backbone and flattened
black pepper

MARINADE
125 mL (½ cup) olive oil
3 cloves garlic, chopped
2 tablespoons rosemary leaves
2 tablespoons lemon juice

To make the marinade, combine all the ingredients, pour over the quail and allow to marinate for a few hours.

Heat the barbecue or grill and cook the quail, adding a little black pepper as you go. A dash of good-quality Thai fish sauce may do the job in place of salt, and adds a new flavour dimension. Fish sauce and rosemary may seem at odds, but they work well together. Do not overcook the quail. Get used to the idea that a little pinkness will not kill you and that the food will be more succulent.

COZZE AL LEMONGRASS E PEPERONCINO

STEAMED MUSSELS WITH LEMONGRASS AND CHILLI

The humble mussel is a pillar of Italian cooking. It is not a very celebrated mollusc in Australia, but it is always fairly available due to the many mussel farms. It is also inexpensive. For me, it is a great starter to an informal meal with friends who are not scared to slurp and to dip their bread into the marine juices of this dish.

The beauty of this recipe — which is neither regional nor original — is that the subtle flavour of lemongrass combines well with traditional ingredients like tomatoes, basil and garlic. Like many of these ad hoc dishes, precise quantities are more to do with intuition than precision.

The distinctive seawater taste of this dish reminds me of a funny but true story about a peasant dish in the Apulia region known as 'the fish that got away'. To obtain that essence of the sea in the absence of a real catch, the poor were known to boil small rocks collected from the bottom of the sea, especially those that had a little green growth on them. The addition of vegetables, garlic and basil were supposed to finish this soup.

Serves 4

PREPARATION TIME: 30 MINUTES

COOKING TIME: 5 MINUTES

3 tablespoons olive oil, preferably extra-virgin

3 cloves garlic, coarsely chopped

2 cm (¾ inch) ginger, coarsely chopped

3 sticks lemongrass, coarsely chopped

2 red chillies, coarsely chopped

parsley leaves and stalks, coarsely chopped

a few pieces lemon peel, coarsely chopped

1 kg (2 lb) mussels, beards removed

80 mL (⅓ cup) good-quality white wine

Heat the oil in a saucepan and rapidly add the garlic, ginger, lemongrass, chillies, parsley and lemon peel. Add the mussels at once and, with the flame on high, place a lid over the saucepan. After a moment or two, add the white wine and cover again. It will only take a few moments for the mussels to steam open. Shake the pan to help them along. Those that stubbornly refuse to open should be discarded. (It may pay to remove the great bulk of cooked ones before attempting to open the tough one.)

The mussels should be fragrant, redolent of lemongrass and, above all, juicy. Do not overcook, ever.

POLIPO AFFOGATO IN OLIO

OCTOPUS IN OIL

In Australia we can still buy gigantic octopus at a fairly reasonable price. The Greek community makes great use of it, whereas the Italians tend to go for calamari or smaller octopus. This is a recipe for giant octopus that I learnt from Cheong Liew's book, My Food. *He says he learnt it from the Greeks. Either way, it's delicious. The octopus slices can be served as antipasto. The juices, with the addition of tomatoes, make a superlative pasta sauce.*

Serves 6

PREPARATION TIME: 30 MINUTES

COOKING TIME: 30 MINUTES

2 kg (4 lb) octopus, tenderised
1 L (4 cups) extra-virgin olive oil
4 anchovies
2 heads garlic, cut in half
2 long red chillies

Clean the octopus by removing its beak and suckers — some people leave them on, but I do not like them. Please yourself if you have a position on this. I also remove some of the skin.

Bring the oil, anchovies, garlic and chilli to almost smoking point in a pot and slowly immerse the octopus in and out so as to not lose the heat in the pot. After a few dunkings, place the octopus in the pot. Put a lid on and cook on the lowest flame possible. It will be soft and ready to eat after about 30 minutes.

Remove the octopus from the oil and slice. Dress with some of the cooking oil and lemon juice, or with a mayonnaise of your choice.

For the use of the leftover cooking liquid for pasta, see page 90.

TO KILL AN OLIVE

Nobody knows how long it takes to kill an olive.
Drought, axe, fire, are admitted failures. Hack one down,
grub out a ton of mainroot for fuel, and next spring
every side-root sends up shoots. A great frost
can leave the trees leafless for years; they revive.
Invading armies will fell them. They return
through the burnt-out ribs of siege machines.

Only the patient goat, nibbling his ways down the ages,
has the malice to master the olive. Sometimes, they say,
a man finds a dead orchard, fired and goat-
cropped centuries back. He settles and fences;
the stumps revive. His grandchildren's family prosper
by the arduous oil-pressing trade. The wars
and disease wash over. Goats return. The olives
go under waiting another age.

Their shade still lies where Socrates disputed.
Gethsemane's withered groves are bearing yet.

MARK O'CONNOR

POLENTA E GAMBERI DI FIUME

YABBIES ON GREEN POLENTA

I like the combination of soft polenta and yabbies with the fragrance of a fruity olive oil. This dish is visually attractive and clean in flavour. It is imporant to use the best cheese and olive oil. The polenta has to be creamy, soft and runny.

Serves 6

PREPARATION TIME: 30 MINUTES
COOKING TIME: 30 MINUTES

30 cooked and peeled yabbies (see note)

3 cups polenta (cornmeal)

1 cup grated Parmigiano Reggiano

salt

water

1 cup finely chopped young spinach or continental (flat leaf) parsley

125 mL (½ cup) extra-virgin olive oil

Shell the yabbies and set aside.

Bring 2 L (8 cups) lightly salted water to the boil. Add the polenta in a steady stream, stirring all the time until all the flour has been incorporated and there are no lumps. Add the cheese and adjust to taste with salt. Cook for 30 minutes, and if the mixture looks like drying out, add more water. Add the spinach or parsley last, just before dishing up, to keep the colour. Add more for a greener effect.

Spoon the polenta into bowls, and divide the yabbies between them. Drizzle generously with the olive oil and serve.

A NOTE ABOUT YABBIES

It is better to buy live yabbies. Drop them in plenty of hot water with the usual aromatics — parsley, peppercorns, celery, onion, lemongrass, lemon and so on. Cook for 5 minutes, and drain. Do not refresh.

POLIPO E PATATE

OCTOPUS WITH POTATOES

The same giant octopus from page 50 can be cooked in boiling water with aromatics such as root vegetables and herbs. Cook to the degree of tenderness you like, but beware of making it too mushy. Some Italians belive that when boiling octopus the addition of a few wine corks in the water will help to tenderise it. I suppose you can try!

Serves 6

COOKING TIME: 30 MINUTES

2 bay leaves
1 tablespoon black peppercorns
1 stalk celery
1 onion
parsley stalks
250 mL (1 cup) white wine
2 kg (4 lb) octopus
6 potatoes
1 handful green beans
olive oil
salt and pepper
lemon juice

Bring water, the aromatics and wine to the boil in a medium-sized heavy-based pot (how much water needed to just cover the octopus depends on the size of your pot). Once the water comes to the boil, plunge in the octopus, then lift out of the pot. Allow the water to come to the boil again, then repeat.

When the water comes back to the boil again, add the octopus, lower the heat and cook until it is tender.

Steam the potatoes until cooked. Blanch the beans in some boiling water, then refresh in cool water.

When the octopus is tender, remove from the pot and slice the tentacles and head on an angle.

To serve, slice the potatoes and place on the base of serving plates. Add the beans, then the octopus, and dress to taste with olive oil, salt, pepper and lemon juice.

BACCALÀ MANTECATO

CREAMED COD

Serves 8 as an antipasto

PREPARATION TIME: SOAKING FISH FOR 2 DAYS — IT DOES NOT SMELL — AND 45 MINUTES TO ASSEMBLE

600 g (1¼ lb) baccalà (salted cod)

1 L (4 cups) milk

2 L (8 cups) water

5 peppercorns

2 bay leaves

1 clove garlic, finely chopped

250 mL (1 cup) flavoursome but light olive oil

1 medium-sized boiled potato,
peeled and chopped

a few drops of lemon juice

a pinch of black pepper

a pinch of chopped parsley

You will need to soak the baccalà in cold water for 2 days, changing the water frequently.

Place the cod in a pot with the milk, water, peppercorns and bay leaves and gently bring to the boil. Simmer for a few minutes and remove from the heat. Let the cod cool to the point where you can handle the flesh. Remove the bones, skin and other hard bits, especially towards the tail end.

Place the flaked fish in a food processor with the garlic. Give it a few quick turns to break it down and begin to add the oil as if making a mayonnaise. Add the potato and incorporate well with a few more turns. Keep going with the oil and a few drops of lemon juice until you have a mixture of soft consistency. Taste to be sure that all the elements have come together well. If you feel there is enough oil do not add more: you should not have to use the whole cup. At this final stage add 1–2 tablespoons of chilled water; the water will emulsify the oil and make the mixture look lighter in colour.

Sprinkle with a little fresh black pepper and the parsley and serve with grilled yellow polenta or bruschetta.

CROCHETTE DI BACCALÀ
BACCALÀ CROQUETTES

Any leftover baccalà mantecato can be deep-fried. The mixture is already firm due to the presence of potatoes. All you have to do is to shape it into fingers or little balls, roll them in flour, egg and breadcrumbs. Fry until golden and serve with a mayonnaise.

VENETO UPBRINGING

LORETTA SARTORI

I am the daughter of migrants from the Veneto, although I was born and raised in Melbourne with the Australian version of the Italian upbringing. As the daughter of migrants, fragments of their experiences became the foundation of my understanding of Italian culture and some of its traditions. For instance, how could a religious ceremony be complete without the presence of a large cake or multiple small cakes? Knowing with certainty that your host wished to impress by offering the latest release from the cellar, it is a foregone conclusion that you bring an offering of biscuits or *paste* (small cakes) from the local *pasticceria* (cake shop) in order to allow the charade to continue as planned.

How could a feast day pass without the cooking of a particular meal or at the very least a toast to the saint in question at the local bar or among friends in a private home? How could the change of seasons not have celebrations surrounding the latest produce, including gatherings to pickle, preserve, bake, slaughter or harvest in unison? Even though we are relocated, the traditions are adhered to so that we may keep our connection with Italy.

Memories that give insight to my heritage go back to my paternal grandfather, who lived out his days on a small apple orchard with two cows, a dog called Rover, who responded well to the Veneto dialect, and a glorious vegetable garden. As with many other cultures, the bond of food was imperative. I can recall snatched weekends during summer at Nonno's, sitting beneath the cherry tree, reaching upwards lazily for a handful of warm plump fruit, the sweetness of which is sometimes difficult to recapture. Or reaching across to the gooseberry hedge. When all of this became too dull for a four-year-old, I took a short meander to the strawberry patch to savour the golfball-sized berries.

Meanwhile, the adults were happily ensconced beneath the burdened grapevine, enjoying the shade and the fruit juices (now alcoholic) from last year's crop. Nonno would always scold us if we jumped up to snatch a grape, insisting that it had to be a bunch or none at all. That wasn't such a difficult penalty as our preferred choice was the delicious *fragola* (strawberry-scented) grape, whose distinctive elongated shape was easy to spot.

In winter the sweetness of the air subsided, to be replaced with the early morning smell of coffee, laced with grappa for the menfolk and milk for the women and children. Homemade continental sausages splattered and sizzled directly on the wood stove. These were cooked 'crunchy' for the younger ones and sandwiched between coarsely cut pieces of wood-fired bread. This substantial feast gave us sufficient energy to pursue the morning's activities, one of the more popular being mushrooming.

The bounty of saucer-sized field funghi led to a hearty meal cooked with polenta, the staple from our beloved Veneto.

I can happily recall my grandfather's 'milk closet', where the fresh milk was stored after he milked the two cows. The yield was sufficient to supply his needs and those of two families. It wasn't so much the milk that we children were interested in, as the cream that developed after settling. This cream was transferred to a tall, glass cylindrical vessel and was so thick that the large silver spoon would remain upright without touching the bottom. We lavished the cream onto fresh wood-fired bread with the jam that Mum had made using strawberries collected from the garden.

And as for cheese, my father always purchased a full round of cheddar which would last us a long time, no doubt due to the cloth in which it was initially set and the linen bag that my mother made for storage. I can still recall the 'bite' and texture!

FILETTI DI PESCE AL LIMONE

LEMON-CURED FISH

*For this refreshing antipasto you can use any firm-fleshed fish or prawns. In an ideal world
I'd suggest Murray perch, but any other fish will do. Surprisingly, sardines, neither white
nor firm, once filleted, are very good.*

*I remember eating prawns cured in vinegar at a lunch at the Hilton in Kuching.
This is a variation based on that memory. Here, vinegar is replaced by milder lemon juice.
Acidic or salty teasers should be part of a larger selection of antipasto, so the quantity
given here is rather small. Double it if you wish.*

Serves 4

PREPARATION TIME: 30 MINUTES

300 g (10 oz) firm fish fillet
or firm raw prawns
4 tablespoons lemon juice (or more to taste),
mixed with a little water
1 teaspoon good-quality fish sauce
a pinch of sugar
1 tablespoon finely sliced kaffir lime leaves
1 tablespoon finely chopped red chilli

Make sure the fish is free of bones. Cut into finger-wide
strips if you like.

Mix all the other ingredients and pour over the fish
in a non-reactive dish. Marinate overnight or for at least
5 hours.

SARDINE FRITTE CON L'UOVO

SARDINES IN EGG BATTER

*Sardines, when available fresh, are very good. Sardines have been affected by a virus
resulting, as I understand it, in depleted stocks. It was not long ago that you could see dead
sardines wash up on the western beaches of South Australia. It seems that the fish is now on
its way to recovery. At one point it was possible to buy fresh, just filleted sardines, ready for
many uses. I hope the luxury is soon available to consumers, even though sardines
like that are slightly more expensive.*

*This recipe can be made with frozen sardines. If you buy them whole, decapitate them,
cut them open all the way to the tail and remove the guts and bones. Trim the sides as well
to remove the tiny fins. Rinse to eliminate any scales.*

Serves 4

PREPARATION TIME: 10 MINUTES
COOKING TIME: 5 MINUTES

oil
12 sardines, filleted
plain flour for dusting
4 eggs (or more)
salt and pepper
lemon wedges

Heat the oil for frying in a pan.

Dust the sardines with flour. Beat the eggs lightly
with a pinch of salt and pepper. Immerse the floured
sardines in the eggs and then straight into the oil in
batches of two or three. Fry on both sides. Drain well on
kitchen paper.

There are no breadcrumbs in this recipe, but the egg
should puff up nicely and give more body to the
sardine. Add more salt if necessary, and squeeze over
lemon juice before eating.

ZUPPE

There are two types of soup, if you ask me. One that can be prepared without stock or water, and one that cannot. (Minestrone *can* be made without chicken stock, but it does not taste the same. But let's allow minestrone to equivocate.)

In the first group are those dishes like *zuppa di fave*, thick sludges with pasta, lifted by chilli and olive oil. Such soups are particularly Italian, southern Italian. They rely on a single ingredient with the addition of tomato and pasta or rice. They are cheap to make — even with the addition of the most expensive extra-virgin olive oil or cheese, they are still inexpensive to prepare. You have no excuses but to try.

In the second group are more refined soups — not better, just more worked. Such is the case with many I have listed here; if you need an example, look at *Minestra alla moda di Antonia* (page 69). So, unless you want to stick to the soups in the first group only, you will have to face the music, which is the same over and over again. You will have to stay at home to dedicate some time to stock-making, particularly chicken stock. You can watch television, you can navigate the Internet, you can make love or read stories to the kids while it is happening.

To set up a stock takes only minutes and it will cook itself, mostly. Make extra stock to freeze. Reduce it if you need a concentrated stock for a sauce later. It will take flour and butter and become a classic *velouté*. Either way, if you like food, you'll do stock.

MAKING STOCK

To make CHICKEN STOCK, place a chicken in a pot and cover with cold water. Add, if you wish, one carrot, one onion and a stalk of celery and cook slowly for 2 hours. Skim off any scum as you go to obtain a clear stock. After 2 hours, reduce the stock if you want a stronger flavour. Add salt at the end (if you add it at the start, it might concentrate too much). Remove the meat and vegetables and strain the stock. The meat and vegetables can be reserved for use in a salad.

If you want to capture a 'fresher' flavour, add aromatic vegetables during the last 15 minutes of the cooking time.

To make BEEF STOCK, replace the chicken with brisket, but start off with hot water so that the meat is sealed.

To make FISH STOCK, gently boil 5L (4 quarts) water to which has been added 3 kg (6 lb) fish heads that have been cleaned and 250 mL (1 cup) white wine. Allow to simmer for about 20 minutes. Adjust the strength of the stock by boiling down to concentrate as necessary.

To make VEGETABLE STOCK, combine equal quantities of chopped carrot, onion and celery in a pot and cover with water. Add tomato, a few peppercorns, a bay leaf, parsley stalks and whatever else is compatible. Bring to the boil and allow to simmer for 30 minutes. Strain and reserve the stock, discarding all the vegetables.

ZUPPA DI FAVE E PASTA
BROAD BEAN AND PASTA SOUP

When the fava beans or broad beans are turning from green to yellow, when they seem past their prime, they are ideal for soup. In fact, they are best picked, blanched briefly to remove the outer skin and placed in the freezer in 500 g (1 lb) bags. If you have broad beans in your garden or you have access to them, that may be the time when you are sick and tired of cooking them. After all, you have eaten them for two months in all sorts of ways. Now is the time when the freezer comes in handy. You'll have your rewards later.

Serves 6

PREPARATION TIME: 15 MINUTES

COOKING TIME: 30 MINUTES

2 cups Tomato Sauce (see page 37)
3 cups shelled and skinned broad beans
1 cup small pasta
1 cup grated parmesan
salt and pepper
extra-virgin olive oil

Heat the tomato sauce, add the broad beans and cover with water. Cook until the broad beans are broken up (help break up the beans with a spoon if necessary). The resulting soup should be thick and somewhat grainy.

In another pot cook the pasta in lightly salted boiling water. When the pasta is cooked, tip out nearly all the water: keep 125 mL (½ cup).

Combine the broad beans mixture and the cooked pasta, and finish with cheese, salt and pepper to taste. If you have some really exceptional olive oil, pour 1 tablespoon over each serve of soup, or let diners add as much as they want. This dish is truly a triumph of southern Italian cooking.

PANCOTTO CON PATATE E RUCOLA

BREAD, POTATO AND ROCKET 'SOUP'

I have waxed lyrical about the virtues of old bread — crusty, homemade bread, not thin white slices. It is even a pity to throw the stale bits away. For this recipe it is worth letting some bread go old. The combination of bread and potatoes is, for me, a paradise of starch. This is my variation on Valentina Harris's recipe, which she has taken from the Apulian tradition.

Serves 6

PREPARATION TIME: 1 HOUR

500 g (1 lb) potatoes, peeled and thickly sliced
500 g (1 lb) rocket
300 g (10 oz) crusty old bread
100 mL (3½ fl oz) extra-virgin olive oil
3 cloves garlic, whole
1 red chilli, whole (optional)
salt

Cover the potatoes with cold water in a saucepan and cook until soft. Add the rocket and bread and keep cooking until the bread is quite soft. You may need to add more water to the pot during cooking.

Heat the oil in a pan and fry the garlic and chilli, if using. Discard the chilli. Pour the oil and garlic over the soup. Season with salt.

Traditionally the soup is not served with cheese, but I like to add some strong pecorino.

RISI E BISI

RICE AND PEAS

Risi e bisi, rice and peas, nothing more and nothing less, is a celebrated Venetian dish that I prefer to put under the category of soup rather than risotto. Yes, readers have seen it before, but I am yet to be offered a serve of it anywhere, even though I have lived in Australia for 25 years. So, to repeat may be useful, as the Romans used to say.

Serves 6

COOKING TIME: 50 MINUTES, INCLUDING STOCK-MAKING

1 kg (2 lb) peas in their pods
1 medium-sized carrot, chopped
1 small onion, chopped
1 stalk celery, chopped
olive oil and butter
1 white onion, chopped
100 g (3½ oz) pancetta, thinly sliced and chopped
250 g (8 oz) Italian rice (e.g. vialone)
1 L (4 cups) Chicken Stock (see page 61)
1 cup grated parmesan
black pepper
flat-leaf parsley

Shell the peas and reserve the pods for the stock. Combine the pods, carrot, onion and celery in a pot and cover with water. Bring to the boil and allow to simmer for 30 minutes. Strain and reserve the stock, discarding all the vegetables.

Heat the oil and butter in a saucepan and sweat the onion. Add the pancetta, then the peas. Cook down a little, then add the rice to gently toast, and start adding the vegetable stock gradually, stirring well between each addition.

When the vegetable stock is finished, use the chicken stock and a little cheese from time to time. Do not let the rice take all the stock. It has to be always a little runny, *all'onda*, as we say — that is, the rice must form a wave when you shake the pot.

When the rice is soft, after 20 minutes, serve at once. Add more cheese and black pepper to taste. I also like to throw in a handful of freshly chopped parsley at the last minute.

ZUPPA DI POMODORO CON POLPETTE DI VITELLO

TOMATO SOUP WITH VEAL MEATBALLS

Perhaps a little fussy, but worth the trouble. If you cannot obtain veal where you live, don't panic. Use chicken or a mixture of chicken and yearling beef. The whole preparation can be made ahead and reheated.

Serves 6

PREPARATION TIME: 40 MINUTES

COOKING TIME: 1 HOUR

SOUP

1 onion, chopped

2 cloves garlic, chopped

olive oil or butter

500 g (1 lb) potatoes, finely sliced (desirée or similar)

2 L (8 cups) Chicken Stock (see page 61)

1 kg (2 lb) ripe tomatoes, seeded and skinned

MEATBALLS

200 g (7 oz) veal

50 g (1½ oz) breadcrumbs

50 g (1½ oz) parmesan, grated

2 eggs

salt and pepper

2 L (8 cups) Chicken Stock (see page 61)

To make the soup, fry the onion and garlic in a small amount of oil or butter or a mixture of both in a stockpot until they take on a some colour. Add the potatoes and a some stock to moisten and cook until soft.

Add the tomato pulp and cook on a low heat until the potatoes are soft, adding more stock if necessary. This may take more than 1 hour.

To make the meatballs, combine all the ingredients except the stock. Roll one or two into meatballs and test by cooking in a little simmering water — if they are too soft and fall apart, add more egg and cheese. When they float to the top and remain firm, proceed with the rest of the mixture.

Heat the stock in a saucepan, reduce to a gentle simmer and cook the meatballs in batches. When they float to the top, ladle out and set aside. Reserve the stock.

Pass the potato and tomato soup through a fine sieve. Thin out with more stock (or use the stock you used to cook the *polpette*) if the mixture is too thick. The potato and tomato soup shouldn't be too thin or broth-like, however.

To serve, reheat the soup gently in a saucepan. Add the *polpette* to warm through, then serve.

BRODO ALLA BOLOGNESE
BOLOGNESE BROTH

Good food is often based on your understanding of how simple things can give the best results. This traditional soup comes from the Romagna region and is similar to stracciatella. *I like the soup's simplicity and its comforting qualities during the winter months. It is essential to have a good stock made from some chicken, beef bones and a flavoursome cut of meat like brisket. The brisket and the chicken can be eaten with a salad after the soup.*

Serves 6

PREPARATION AND COOKING TIME: 20 MINUTES

2 L (8 cups) Chicken Stock (see page 61)
2 L (8 cups) Beef Stock (see page 61)
5 eggs
180 g (6 oz) parmesan, grated
100 g (3½ oz) breadcrumbs

Combine the stocks and bring to a boil and reduce by half. This intensifies the flavours.

Mix the eggs with the parmesan and breadcrumbs. With the stock on a gentle simmer, add the egg mixture and cook until it just sets, stirring occasionally. Eat at once.

MINESTRONE FREDDO ALLA MILANESE

COLD MINESTRONE SOUP MILANESE-STYLE

Minestrone can be eaten hot or cold. Many Australians who live in hot climates miss out on this great dish and many more because of their obstinate love for food served hot. I must say, however, that in recent times I have noticed a shift toward a greater acceptance of foods served at room temperature.

This recipe is for a standard minestrone to be eaten at room temperature. Use whatever greens you have or find compatible. You can enhance the flavour of the minestrone by adding prosciutto skin or parmesan crusts.

Serves 10

PREPARATION TIME: 1 HOUR

COOKING TIME: 1½ HOURS

100 g (3½ oz) potatoes
100 g (3½ oz) zucchini
100 g (3½ oz) carrots
100 g (3½ oz) asparagus
100 g (3½ oz) green beans
1 small celery heart
100 g (3½ oz) butter
1 medium-sized red onion, thinly sliced
200 g (7 oz) preferably fresh tomatoes, peeled and seeded
100 g (3½ oz) peas
100 g (3½ oz) borlotti or cannellini beans, soaked overnight
3 L (12 cups) Chicken or Vegetable Stock (see page 61)
200 g (7 oz) Italian rice (e.g. vialone)
salt and pepper
parmesan

Chop the potatoes, zucchini, carrots, asparagus, green beans and celery heart into uniform pieces.

Melt the butter in a large stockpot and sauté the onions, carrots and potatoes. Add the tomatoes and then all the other vegetables and beans. Sweat them for a little while and when all the vegetables are well integrated, add the stock. Cook until the vegetables are tender.

Add the rice and continue to cook over a low heat until *al dente*. Season to taste with salt and pepper. Stop the cooking — or else the rice will continue to expand — and spread the minestrone in a large baking dish or similar so that it cools rapidly. You can even pour it into a number of soup bowls and allow to sit until it's time to serve. When you do, sprinkle generously with the best parmesan. You can also add a tablespoon of pesto to the soup.

MINESTRA ALLA MODA DI ANTONIA

SOUP IN THE STYLE OF ANTONIA

Antonia is my olive oil-maker friend Gianni Grigoletto's mother. Although it appears a little fussy, this lovely soup is easy to prepare. The result is elegant and particularly suited to the long, cold winter months we get in southern Australia.

To make a good soup, you must have a good chook, or at least some parts of it, like the wings and the feet. There are as many schools of thought on stock as there are chefs. I have tested and retested my beliefs, and am happy to confirm that, for the best results, gently, gently boil the chicken with some root vegetables and a little salt, skimming as you go.

Serves 4

PREPARATION TIME: 40 MINUTES

2 eggs
2 tablespoons grated parmesan
4 slices mortadella or cooked ham, finely chopped
1 tablespoon plain (all-purpose) flour
salt and pepper
2 tablespoons melted butter
a little grated nutmeg
2 L (8 cups) Chicken Stock (see page 61)

Beat the eggs with the cheese, add the mortadella or ham and the flour. Season with salt and pepper, add the butter and nutmeg, and place the mixture in the bottom third of a clean tea-towel and roll up so it looks like a salami.

Bring the stock to the boil and reduce the heat to a gentle simmer. Place the rolled-up tea-towel in the pot and allow to cook in the stock for 30 minutes or less.

Take out the roll and allow it to cool. The soup can be done well ahead to this point.

When ready to serve, chop the solidified mixture into little cubes. Bring the stock back to the boil and add the cubed mixture. Allow to warm up, then serve at once, with more cheese if desired.

POLLO E SCAROLA

CHICKEN AND ENDIVE SOUP

A soup I learnt from my relatives who came to Australia from the ancient town of Montemurro in southern Italy. I am sure this dish was invented to dispose of some old boilers, but it works well with any chicken. It is labour intensive, but not fraught with technical difficulties.

Serves 6

PREPARATION AND COOKING TIME: 2 HOURS

1 × 1.7 kg (3½ lb) chicken, whole
1 onion, whole
1 stalk celery, whole
1 carrot, whole
2 bunches curly endive or young silverbeet
1 cup grated pecorino
2 eggs
½ cup breadcrumbs
salt and pepper

Place the chicken, onion, celery and carrot in a pot and cover with water. Boil over low heat until a clear stock is achieved and the chicken is well cooked, about 1 hour or more. Reserve the stock.

Remove the meat from the chicken and place in a food processor. Mince to a fine paste and set aside.

Wash the endive or silverbeet in plenty of water and blanch in salted water until tender. Chill in a bath of iced water (this is not strictly necessary). Squeeze as much water as possible out of the greens, chop coarsely and set aside.

Add cheese, eggs and breadcrumbs to the chicken and mix to obtain a firm paste. Add salt and pepper to taste. Roll one or two into meatballs and test by cooking in a little simmering water — if they are too soft and fall apart, add more egg and cheese. When they float to the top and remain firm, proceed with the rest of the mixture. Roll into tiny balls, then poach them in the stock and set aside. When you are ready to eat, reheat the stock and add the greens and the chicken balls.

Divide between serving bowls, and offer more cheese and salt if needed for flavour.

FREGOLA CON BRODO DI PESCE, GAMBERI O VONGOLE

PASTA IN BROTH WITH FISH, PRAWNS OR CLAMS

Fregola is a Sardinian pasta. This tiny pasta, half the size of a grain of rice, is actually roasted after drying. When cooked, it swells up and reminds me of couscous. Perhaps the Saracens, who roamed the Mediterranean in pirate ships, left some of their culinary legacy on this sunny and mysterious ancient island.

Fregola is superlative when combined with seafood, and is traditionally served with clams — which is fantastic if you are prepared to tolerate the odd grain of sand. Given the unreliability of Australian clams — they are often too sandy and not suspended in sea-water long enough for the sand to be expelled — I cook fregola with fish stock to which I add bits of seafood. If you have uncooked prawn heads, make a stock with these first, and add the prawn meat at the end.

The addition of a fragrant olive oil to the dish makes this dish even more attractive. Or try shellfish oil. The dish should have the consistency of a runny soup, the texture of couscous, and the deep flavour of the sea.

Serves 6

PREPARATION TIME: 1 HOUR
COOKING TIME: 10 MINUTES

2 L (8 cups) Fish Stock (see page 61)
500 g (1 lb) fregola
fruity extra-virgin olive oil
1 cup mussel meat and any leftover juices
from ½ kg (1 lb) mussels
parsley
12 raw prawns, shelled and deveined
½ cup grated pecorino

Bring the stock to the boil and drop in the fregola. Cook until soft, 7–8 minutes, then take off the heat. The fregola will drink up the stock, puff up, and the mixture will become slightly runny.

To open the mussels, heat some olive oil in a pan, add the mussels and a handful of parsley. Cover with a lid and cook until they barely open. This can be done ahead of time. Remove the meat from the shells. Reserve any leftover cooking juices.

Seal the prawns in some olive oil in a frying pan on both sides.

To serve, combine the fregola with the seafood, toss and add the cheese. Add the mussel juices to thin out if the mixture is too gluggy.

RISOTTI

Many people know about cooking risotto these days, such is its popularity, but the method is worth repeating. To a base — usually a little onion or onion and vegetables, which have been cooked according to the recipe — add the rice. The action of stirring the rice with the base — and that sometimes can just be a little bit of onion — is called 'toasting' the rice. The rice is ready for the next stage when it shows signs of sticking to the bottom of the pan.

Add the stock, little by little, until the rice is *al dente*. Some cooks finish the rice with butter. That action is called *'mantecare'*, which can render the rice creamy or too rich, depending on your perspective. I do it with some risotto and not with others, especially not with those that may accompany another dish or have a rich base such as sausage.

I also like to add a tiny bit of lemon zest to the finished dish. Most of the time it imparts an attractive citrus dimension that cuts through the richness. However, this dimension must be very, very light, almost imperceptible.

Some risotti have a light base of onion and garlic and are not finished with the main ingredient until the end. This is to prevent spoiling delicate flavours such as scallops, prawns, crab and other seafood or vegetables that may discolour, such as zucchini, asparagus or spinach.

I insist on a good stock of chicken, beef, a combination of both, or fish (see page 61 for stocks). A piece of brisket and a chook will give you separately or together a great stock. The chicken and the brisket, although soft after prolonged cooking, can still be used for a salad. If you add a carrot, an onion and a stalk of celery, all these overcooked vegetables combined with the meats make a tasty salad if you have a good olive oil and a sound red wine vinegar.

You have to look for flavour wherever you can get it. I have learnt to use the pods of peas or the stems of asparagus to extract flavour for a risotto. Prawn heads or crab carcasses can be used in the same way.

A vegetable stock is necessary for vegetarian dishes. For a vegetarian stock, I use chopped root vegetables so that they will release their flavour quickly, without overcooking. Tomatoes and other vegetable trimmings will help to improve the flavour of the risotto.

RISOTTO CON SNAPPER E FINOCCHIO

SNAPPER AND FENNEL RISOTTO

I love any risotto that somehow incorporates fish. Here I want to cook the fillets separately and make a risotto to accompany them. This risotto must be flavoured with a compatible vegetable, such as fennel.

Serves 4

PREPARATION TIME: 40 MINUTES

COOKING TIME: 20 MINUTES

1 whole snapper, about 1.2 kg (2 lb 7 oz)

SNAPPER STOCK

1 onion, chopped

4 tablespoons butter

125 mL (½ cup) extra-virgin olive oil

trimmings and head from the snapper

4 parsley stalks

1 bay leaf

125 mL (½ cup) white wine

2 L (8 cups) Fish Stock (see page 61)

RISOTTO

extra-virgin olive oil

1 bulb fennel, diced (reserve the tips for decoration)

2 cloves garlic, chopped

2 cups arborio rice

1 cup grated pecorino

salt and pepper

1 cup diced fresh tomato

GREEN PARSLEY OIL

125 mL (½ cup) olive oil

1 cup parsley

2 anchovy fillets

Get your fishmonger to fillet the snapper, but reserve the head, the bones and other trimmings. Use them to intensify the flavour of the fish stock. Heat some butter and oil in a pot and fry off the onion. Add the snapper head and other trimmings, the parsley, bay leaf and white wine. Add the fish stock. Cook for a few minutes, pressing down occasionally to get out as much juice as possible. Put the mixture through a fine sieve, discarding the solids. Bring the reserved stock to a gentle simmer in a separate saucepan.

To make the risotto, heat some oil in a pan over a gentle heat. Cook the fennel and garlic. Do not colour — the risotto has to be delicate and white. Add the rice and stir. Slowly add the stock, ladle by ladle, stirring to make sure all the stock is absorbed between each addition. Continue until the stock is used up. The rice should be *al dente*. Add the pecorino, salt and pepper.

In the meantime, seal the fillets in a frying pan in a little oil and butter. Finish the cooking in an oven preheated to 180°C (350°F).

To make the green parsley oil, blend the oil, parsley and anchovies in a blender and mix until well combined. Push through a fine strainer.

Place the risotto on a big platter. Scatter with chopped fennel leaves and tomato. Place the fish fillets around (break them down if you like). Spoon the green parsley oil here and there.

THE ECONOMY OF SCALE

Once you get the idea of this risotto, the applications are as many as there is fish. This is a preparation worth talking about, because it results in a dish that has rice and fish in one. Many of us, these days, have limited time to cook and therefore single dishes incorporating two or even three elements are useful ways to save time. With a salad to round off the meal, one gets all the elements of nutrition and fun in a matter of a few minutes.

Also, rice is cheap, fish is not. By combining rice and fish, you can stretch the budget, especially when you want to entertain friends without taxing your pocket too much. I have gone out to buy this and that for a small dinner party, and by the time I was finished, the best part of a hundred dollars had evaporated, and that was before buying any reasonable wine.

This dish works out to about two dollars for rice, twenty to thirty for fish, six for bread, ten for salad and ten for everything else. (In everything else I include herbs, which goes to show how much money you can save if you have a little herb garden or a few pots with the basics.) I can entertain four or five people with a good risotto, fish and a salad and some bread at about twelve dollars per person, give or take. If you are prepared to scale down the cost of fish by using something like trevally or skate, the cost will be even less. The point of eating together is not always to savour a gastronomic revelation; it is to socialise.

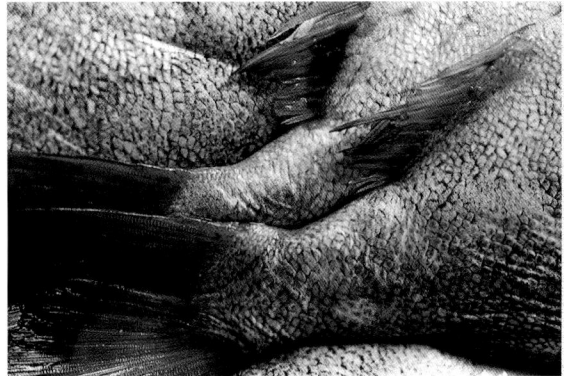

RISOTTO CON GRANCHIO E ZUCCHINE

RISOTTO WITH CRAB AND ZUCCHINI

Zucchini are almost tasteless, but provide great colour and texture, which is why I like them with seafood. Crabmeat is also very delicate, so to obtain a good risotto you need the best of Australian blue swimmer crabs. And patience, because you have to cook the crabs and extract the meat yourself. You also need a clean fish stock; it has to be flavoursome, but very clean.

The crabs must be very fresh. Even a light trace of bad smell must be regarded with utter suspicion. Bring a pot of water to the boil with vegetable trimmings such as celery, onion peelings, garlic skins (or a full clove), parsley stalks and other aromatics of your choice. Pull the tops off the crabs and remove the innards. Add the crabs for about 5 minutes or until cooked. Let them cool. Extract the meat by cutting through the shell and cartilage with scissors.

Serves 4

PREPARATION TIME: 1 HOUR

COOKING TIME: 20 MINUTES

6 large crabs, cooked

8 tablespoons olive oil

2 cloves garlic, smashed

2 L (8 cups) light Fish Stock (see page 61)

300 g (10 oz) Italian rice

250 mL (1 cup) white wine

salt and pepper

2 tablespoons butter

200 g (7 oz) zucchini, cut into very small pieces

grated lemon zest

fresh parsley

grated parmesan

Extract the meat from the crabs and set aside. Reserve the shells.

Heat half of the oil, add the garlic and crab shells. Toast, and when the shells have changed colour, add a ladle or two of fish stock. Stir and reduce to extract as much flavour from the shells as possible. Strain off the juices, gently reduce to a glaze and set aside.

Bring the stock to the boil.

Toast the rice in the remaining oil. Add the wine, and once it has evaporated, add the fish stock, stirring between each addition until the stock is all used up and the rice is *al dente*. Taste for salt and pepper.

Melt the butter in a separate pan and toss the zucchini for 1 minute. Add the zucchini to the risotto and finish by adding the crabmeat, lemon zest, parsley and cheese.

Serve the rice and spoon over some reduced sauce. If you don't care for that, tip the sauce into the risotto and mix it in before serving.

RISOTTO PRIMAVERA

SPRING RISOTTO

Here is a fresh risotto, particularly good when asparagus are abundant and crispy fresh. You can exploit asparagus and other vegetables for beautiful combinations that celebrate the arrival of spring.

I like to serve this risotto with lightly cooked asparagus arranged on a plate with their spears pointing out, the risotto on top in the centre, and finish with the finest julienne of pumpkin and red capsicum. A sauce made with a light purée of pumpkin and fresh tomato can surround the mound of risotto. The idea is to create a healthy and happy-looking dish that is both pleasant to look at and to eat.

Serves 6

PREPARATION TIME: 1 HOUR

COOKING TIME: 20 MINUTES

2 L (8 cups) Vegetable Stock (see page 61)

lemon zest

olive oil

butter

1 red onion, chopped

3 spring onions, white part only, chopped

½ cup diced potatoes

2½ cups arborio rice

½ cup peas

½ cup diced zucchini

½ cup diced tomatoes

grated parmesan

salt and pepper

18 asparagus spears

pumpkin, finely julienned

red capsicum (bell pepper), finely julienned

Prepare the stock following the instructions on page 61. After you have strained the stock, and while it is still warm, add the lemon zest and allow to infuse.

Heat some olive oil and butter in a pan and cook the red onion and spring onions until soft. Add the potatoes and cook until soft, then add the rice and 'toast' it.

Gradually add the warm stock, peas, zucchini and tomatoes. Keep adding the stock, a ladleful at a time, stirring between each addition until the stock is absorbed. Continue until the rice is *al dente*, then add the cheese. Season with salt and pepper and add a little of the best olive oil you have. Let it rest a minute.

Blanch the asparagus in some boiling water and cool in ice water. Divide the asparagus spears between serving plates and place a serve of risotto alongside. Top with a julienne of pumpkin and red capsicum.

If you wish to make a pumpkin sauce, cook a cup of diced pumpkin in a little stock with a clean piece of pork skin, a bay leaf, a clove of garlic and ½ cup grated parmesan. When cooked (about 10 minutes) pass through a sieve and dilute with olive oil. In a food processor, blend some tomato flesh to a purée. Spread the pumpkin sauce on the plate and dot with small drops of tomato purée. Scatter fresh, small basil leaves all around, place the asparagus on top, followed by the risotto and the garnish of julienned pumpkin and red capsicum.

ITALIAN WINES

I love Australian wines, but I must hasten to say that often they have a punch-up with Italian-style food. Not always, but often. You have to choose wines that are not over-wooded and with some crisp acidity to accompany Italian food. Riesling comes immediately to mind, as long as it is not too aromatic or kerosene-like.

The area I live in produces the bulk of Australian wine exported to the world. If it is good enough for the English and the Germans, I do not see why it is not good enough for Australians. Here, you find some wines with light wood treatment, and they do not punish the pocket either. Many solid commercial labels contain wines that have been generated by grapes grown in the Murray Valley. Anybody with a little honesty in the wine industry will confirm that. Often light and fresh, they are fine with some Italian food. And there will be more variety coming out of this area in the years ahead.

Imported Italian whites often disappoint the Australian palate, because they are either not wooded, not in-your-face fruit-driven, or because they may not be up to scratch. Many Australian wine critics do not understand these wines, even less their function in gastronomy. One variety, which I think will do well in Australia, called Vermentino, is often described as 'inferior' by local scribes, when actually it is an ideal accompaniment for spicy/salty southern Italian foods like anchovies, tuna, *bottarga* and *bottarga di tonno*. Beware of critics who tell you that only Garganega — which makes Soave — and a couple of others are good. They are, undoubtedly, but they are not the only ones.

It is a little harder to find Australian reds that are elegant without being pricey or that are not too overpowering, although dishes like osso buco and other slow-cooked dishes can take a lot of wine power.

Australia is beginning to produce some Italian varieties like Sangiovese and Nebbiolo.

In Euston, near Mildura, Chalmer's Nurseries, which supplies about 40 per cent of all vines in Australia, is releasing a set of new varieties: Sagrantino from Umbria, Schioppettino from Friuli, new clones of Sangiovese, Barbera and Nebbiolo, and many more. These vines are not going to replace those that have worked here for a long time, but will add variety and meet new ways of eating.

If money is no object, or your curiosity is bigger than your wallet, by all means go and have a look at some imported Nebbiolos and Barberas. Talk with a reliable merchant to find all the facts, because these wines are really exposed to the quality of the vintage. I believe that Chianti, fun as it is and good as it is, is not truly representative of Italian wines in the same way that any French region is not representative of another French region. Unfortunately, in the mind of Australian consumers, Chianti is Italy's finest expression of wine, but Italian wines are a lot more than Chianti.

There are many books in English if you want to study this subject, and a large number of well-informed merchants who know their onions. Enoteca Sileno in Melbourne began importing good Italian wines when the names of Italian wines were still dirty words. They sell directly to the public. David Ridge in Adelaide has one of the most interesting portfolios of Italian wines in Australia. David Trembath in Melbourne has single-handedly caused a revolution in thinking by tirelessly promoting food and Italian wine. Major merchants are Negociants in all capital cities, Seabrook Tucker in all capital cities, Dorado (Melbourne) and Arquila Wines (Sydney and Melbourne). There are many more, but these are a good starting point.

Do not forget the range of wines by Gary Crittenden, who went out on a limb a long time ago with a range called I. Gary took a big risk and gave us very attractive, sometimes outstanding, wines made from Italian clones for a very reasonable price. He has also supported growers in their efforts to understand how to deal with these unknown varieties.

RISOTTO AL VINO ROSSO

RISOTTO OF RED WINE

I think this is a great risotto, although I concede that it may be an acquired pleasure —
not everyone finds the taste of wine appealing. I like it as a celebration of vintage
and the onset of autumn.

I agree with American wine writer Matt Kramer's sentiment that instead of the traditional
Barolo wine — now too expensive — it is better to use a 'drinkable' cabernet. Kramer also
suggests using some bone marrow with this risotto, and I could not agree more. Kramer's
A Passion for Piedmont is one of the best, if not the best, book in the English language on the
cuisine of a region. (Bravo, Matt! Your wine notes should be read by all those who want to
understand the secret of the Nebbiolo grape and other Piedmontese varieties.)

I would not hesitate serving this risotto with a grilled pork sausage or with
braised ox cheek if I wanted a 'complete' meal.

Serves 4

PREPARATION TIME: 15 MINUTES
COOKING TIME: 20 MINUTES

1.5 L (6 cups) Beef Stock (see page 61)
butter
60 g (2 oz) bone marrow
1 onion, finely chopped
2 cups arborio rice
750 mL (3 cups) cabernet (not too heavy)
1 tablespoon tomato paste
pepper
parmesan

Bring the stock to the boil.

Melt some butter in a saucepan and fry the bone marrow. Add the onion and cook until soft. Add the rice and 'toast' it. Add a ladle of stock to the rice — do not drown the rice or it will cook too quickly — and add another when the first has been absorbed. Continue, alternating a little wine with a little stock.

When the rice is *al dente*, add the tomato paste, a little pepper and some cheese. Taste and adjust the seasoning; aim to keep the flavours in balance.

RISOTTO DI FEGATINI
RISOTTO WITH CHICKEN LIVERS

You'll go to bed warm, happy and contented after this meal — this is as good as risotto gets!

I make a very rich ragù *of chicken livers and giblets in much the same way as a bolognese, then I prepare a plain white risotto with cheese and a little freshly grated nutmeg. I place a good quantity of* ragù *on the bottom of a baking dish, cover it with the risotto, sprinkle on top the finest breadcrumbs mixed with cheese and chopped sage, and bake for a few moments until golden. Winter food, no doubt, and what a treat!*

Serves 6–8

PREPARATION TIME: 1 HOUR

COOKING TIME: 5–6 MINUTES

SAUCE

1 cup equal quantities of chopped onions, carrots and celery

2 cloves garlic, chopped

olive oil

300 g (10 oz) chicken livers, washed and minced

200 g (7½ oz) chicken giblets, washed and finely minced

2 bay leaves

400 g (14 oz) canned tomatoes

2 tablespoons tomato paste

salt and pepper

2 L (8 cups) Chicken Stock (see page 61)

1 large onion, chopped

2 cloves garlic, left whole

3 cups arborio rice

2 bay leaves

salt and pepper

1 cup breadcrumbs

2 tablespoons freshly chopped sage leaves

grated parmesan

To make the sauce, cook the onion, carrots and celery with the garlic in olive oil until soft and tender. Add the chicken livers, giblets and bay leaves. Cook until there are no juices. Add the tomatoes and tomato paste. Season with salt and pepper and cook until the flavour is well developed, about 1 hour. Check the seasoning again.

In the meantime prepare a white risotto. Bring the stock to the boil. Heat some olive oil in a pan and fry the onion and garlic until fragrant. Add the rice to gently 'toast', then add the bay leaves. Start adding the stock, a ladleful at a time, stirring until each addition is absorbed. Continue until the rice is *al dente*, and season with salt and pepper. Remove the bay leaves and garlic.

Preheat the oven to 180°C (350°F).

Place the sauce in a medium-sized baking dish. Spread the risotto over it. Mix together the breadcrumbs, sage and cheese, sprinkle over the top and bake for 5–6 minutes. Serve hot, at once.

I acquired a taste for chicken livers and other chicken innards when I was a really young child. Any piece of liver in the risotto was called *cicca*, a word that has nothing to do with liver. It was a made-up word. If anything, in dialect, *cicca* was the slang word for a cigarette.

My brother Sergio and I used to compete for the most *cicche*. Sergio was the organist of our village church. I loved going up to the organ stand and mixing with the robust and somewhat out-of-tune country choir. They sang with gusto and joy, so who cares for absolute perfection! So many interpretations of music by the great masters are technically perfect and lack soul. After church, especially on cold days, risotto with *cicche* was almost obligatory.

PASTA

Pasta. Never was there such a loaded word. Not so much for non-Italians who, in a land of plenty like Australia, would be happy to eat spaghetti out of a can. For the Italians, though, it's a special word, with a mythological and religious ring to it. Whether they are business people, public servants, labourers or peasants, they are all committed to this magic carbohydrate. Mothers remind their demanding sons not to be so fussy at the table when they complain of an imperfect pasta dish — how else would they be able to survive the diet imposed by compulsory military service (notorious for being, in the past, a bit revolting)? I did not need to be reminded: any institutional food was enough to make my guts wrench.

When I went to full-day school — 8 am to 5 pm — I was supposed to eat at the school canteen. In retrospect I have no doubt that the nuns who cooked for our school population would have been immaculately clean and committed cooks. I went to the canteen once; the sight of their pasta and the smell of the canteen was the same as having not one finger but five down my throat. From then on I cheated everyone, especially my parents, by never going to lunch there. I'd use the money for morning tea to buy two rolls. I would then pretend to go home for lunch, eat my rolls and pretend again, when everyone returned to class, that I had just come from home. Sometimes I would eat the rolls in the toilet. They were preferable to the canteen. This charade went on for almost a full academic year.

I avoided the military service, by the way, by coming to Australia, and thus did not have a confrontation with mass-produced pasta. What I found in Australia in 1974 was, in parts, worse than military service — but that's another story.

Interestingly, I noticed that in one of his television programs, Antonio Carlucico returned to his Naval Academy in Sardinia. The kitchen there was spotless and the pasta was, with the aid of modern equipment and the expertise of well-trained cooks, mass produced to perfection.

The purpose of my story is to illustrate what a deep and disproportionate psychological influence a bowl of pasta can have on a person's well-being.

Pasta has travelled with migrants through North and South America, Oceania, and throughout Europe. Its simplicity, adaptability and affordability have made it popular the world over. A few friends and a bowl of pasta is often all that is needed to create a happy party, a sense of belonging and good camaraderie.

Italians are so fond of pasta they would easily eat it twice a day. I know for a fact that the *spaghettata* is still one of the most popular ways to get together. A *spaghettata di mezzanotte* is still on the agenda — not so much for young people who, at midnight, are just making ready to go out — but for older people who just do not want to let go of a good day of fun without a parting shot. An improvised *spaghetti aglio e olio* is the way to lift the sagging spirit of a party. Can you say: 'Let's celebrate with a few lamb chops?' And expect the party to lift its spirit? I don't think so. Pasta, for some reason, is happy food. Perhaps that is why it is so popular the world over.

PASTE SECCHE

It is interesting to note that the new laws of the European Economic Community allow pasta to be made with both durum and 'soft' wheat. Furthermore, each style of pasta can be sold without distinction. The new rules are bound to provoke a 'cultural' revolution: will Italians change from pasta *al dente* to a softer type of pasta like Asian noodles?

That question is made even more interesting by yet another related comment by Gianfranco Vissani in the Italian newspaper *La Repubblica*. Signor Vissani, one of Italy's most famous and able chefs, seems to think that as the Italians become more European, they will move away from the traditional *antipasto, primo* and *secondo* structure of the meal in favour of the 'one-dish meal', *piatto unico*. Implicit in this comment is the suggestion that pasta will feature less on the Italian table. He goes on to say, however, that he believes Italians will always have it *al dente*. That is what I call faith!

The one-dish meal, I believe, is already in vogue in Australia. Supplemented by a salad or other vegetables or some cheese or fruit, it is the way to go where time is an expensive commodity. Pasta can play a big role in the one-course meal, as can Asian noodles. In Australia the task is to maintain the division between pasta *al dente* and soft noodles to derive maximum enjoyment from each.

Dry commercial pasta is very good for obvious reasons: it is cheap, portable, lasting and versatile. Where all pasta become tricky is understanding which shape to match to which sauce, and which sauce suits homemade pasta, which is softer because of its egg content and its freshness (homemade pasta can go hard, too, if kept for some time outside the freezer). Here's a list of some types of pasta with a broad indication of their appropriate use.

HARD COMMERCIAL PASTA
SHORT pasta such as tubes of various kinds are good for minestre and minestrone; that is, for chicken broth soups with pasta and vegetables. In broth-based soups, little stars and rice-shaped pasta are appropriate.

SHORT TO MEDIUM This includes penne and rigatoni, shells of various shapes, elbows and many more, usually with an Italian name.

Tomato and cream-based sauces work best. Think of the success, worldwide, of the Roman dish of penne all'arrabbiata. We are not saying that these sauces do not work with other shapes. Quite the contrary. The point is that when you feel like short pasta, you have made a choice of texture almost before the sauce. Hence if you want the texture of penne, then broccoli, tomato and similar vegetables will be appropriate, but not, in my mind, a marinara sauce (with seafood). Short pasta is also useful for salads.

LONG PASTA Spaghetti work well with nearly everything, from raw or cooked vegetables to olive oil and seafood, butter and cheese, pesto and so on. Long pasta such as trenette work well with seafood or pesto as well as rich meaty stews. Linguine work well with clams or fresh tomato or both.

LONG PASTA WITH EGGS When you see fettuccine they are usually all'uovo, with eggs. Not always, but most of the time. All'uovo work well with bolognese and other rich sauces. They also can be broken into a soupy dish of beans such as the celebrated dish pasta e fagioli.

Pappardelle are also long and usually all'uovo. This shape sticks to sauce well. Its porous large surface area is able to suck in a lot of liquid, making it ideal for rabbit stews, chicken livers with cream and so on.

HOMEMADE PASTA
SHORT Rough cuts are short and they suit pulses such as lentils, chickpeas, beans and broad beans. Pork mince (sausage) is also suitable as long as there is some liquid because of their porous nature.

LONG Once again, the same sauces as commercial long pasta apply, but remember that any pasta with eggs is creamy and sticky. Homemade long pasta can take sauces at both ends: light and delicate — butter, seafood, ricotta, vegetarian — as well as rich and flavoursome sauces. Homemade spaghetti and the like can be chilled in cold water for salads, whereas commercial pasta cannot be plunged in cold water without compromising its structure.

PENNE ALLA BOTTARGA DI TONNO

PENNE WITH BOTTARGA

I'd like to introduce readers to the pleasures of bottarga di tonno. Bottarga refers to fish eggs preserved in salt. Usually bottarga refers to the eggs of large grey mullet caught around the Sardinian coast, but not only. These eggs are pressed and when ready, they are sliced and served as an antipasto with lemon juice and oil.

Bottarga is expensive and rare. It is more likely now to come from the African coast, where labour costs are negligible. What can be found in Australia is preserved tuna eggs or tuna bottarga. It is not cheap, but it is worth trying once or twice. I find it addictive, as I have always liked pasta with a salty taste. For this recipe, I suggest you use penne with grooves, which has a pleasant texture.

Serves 4

PREPARATION TIME: 30 MINUTES
COOKING TIME: 20 MINUTES

400 g (14 oz) penne rigate
80 mL (⅓ cup) extra-virgin olive oil
1 cup skinned, seeded and chopped tomatoes
100 g (3½ oz) bottarga di tonno, thinly sliced
4 tablespoons chopped fennel tips
or wild fennel

Cook the penne in plenty of salted water until *al dente*. Drain.

Heat the oil in a pan until warm to hot. Add the tomatoes, then the bottarga, pasta and fennel tips (I do not like dill in this recipe). Serve at once, adding a little extra-virgin olive oil at the table if you desire. Cheese is optional.

SPAGHETTI AL BURRO
SPAGHETTI WITH BUTTER

Spaghetti: to many it is just a word for a dish of something soft, even out of a can. To millions of people, for more than a century, spaghetti has been a magic word, something that simultaneously conjures up happiness and comfort. The sub-categories of those emotions are family, friends, a full stomach, love-making, bright days, festivities. Furthermore, and more pertinently to food itself, one must mention the categories of crunch (known as al dente), perfume (as in the perfume from a pot of boiling spaghetti), and salt and water in balance. The last are crucial: over-treated water has an unpleasant pong; too much salt is just that. The marriage of water and salt is very important, and is of course a matter of personal taste.

How can I be more emphatic? Don't assume that you know how to cook spaghetti — unless you really do. To experiment with balancing the spaghetti act, nothing could be more testing than preparing a bowl of spaghetti al burro — yes, spaghetti with butter and cheese.

This is naked spaghetti. There is no rhetoric here. What you see is what you get. So if it is wrong it will show. Don't be — as I say to my dearest friends — a cockhead: take this seriously, do it well. Your aim is a spaghetti al dente, not oversalted, not too dry or too wet with excess residual water, with the right amount of butter so that it is not too greasy or too dry.

Be careful with cheese: that can also make it dry and the spaghetti will not curl around the fork. The butter must be soft and ready in a bowl, waiting for the spaghetti. Careful if it goes cold, because it could be unappetising.

I don't care if you use salted or unsalted butter. You make that decision, but in my memory I have the flavour of unsalted butter. Another rule: no herbs and no black pepper. There is nothing wrong with either, but that would not be spaghetti al burro.

Serves 4
PREPARATION TIME: 5 MINUTES
COOKING TIME: AS PER COOKING INSTRUCTIONS ON THE PACKET

400 g (14 oz) durum wheat spaghetti
160 g (5½ oz) butter
4 heaped tablespoons grated parmigiano

Allow at least 1 L (4 cups) water for every 100 g (3½ oz) of spaghetti. Bring the salted water to the boil, add the spaghetti and cook following the instructions on the packet. Drain when *al dente*, but save a couple of tablespoons of the cooking water to add at the end to help prevent glugginess

Place the butter in a warm bowl so that it softens. Pour the spaghetti over the butter, add the cheese and mix.

90

SPAGHETTI AL PESTO DI ROSMARINO

SPAGHETTI WITH ROSEMARY PESTO

Most people make pesto with basil and pinenuts. An interesting pesto is one with some rosemary pounded with garlic and cooked briefly in a little butter and oil together with some fresh tomato.

It is the starch in the potatoes and the flavour of the beans that add complexity to the dish. Resist the temptation to cook each separately and add them at the end: it will not be the same.

Serves 6

PREPARATION TIME: 20 MINUTES

COOKING TIME: 20 MINUTES

salt

500 g (1 lb) spaghetti

2 cups diced potatoes

1 cup fresh, chopped green beans

3 tablespoons fresh rosemary needles

4 cloves garlic

125 mL (½ cup) extra-virgin olive oil

2 cups diced fresh tomatoes

1 cup grated parmesan

Bring some salted water to the boil in a pot. Add the spaghetti and the potatoes. Some spaghetti take 7 minutes to cook, which should be enough for the potatoes. Take care to read the instructions on the packet. Two minutes before the spaghetti are ready, add the green beans. Make sure that all the ingredients are perfectly cooked. Drain and set aside.

In the meantime, finely chop the rosemary leaves and pound them with the garlic in a mortar and pestle.

Heat some olive oil in a pan and fry the paste. Add the tomatoes, and cook briefly or until all the aromas have been released.

Toss the sauce with the spaghetti and vegetables, adding extra oil to moisten if necessary. A Ligurian oil, flavoursome and yet delicate, is ideal. Finish with the cheese.

PASTA RICCIA
CON SUGO DI POLIPO
CURLY PASTA WITH TOMATOES AND OCTOPUS

This is a recipe to use up the octopus oil and juices left over from making the antipasto on page 50. For this, I use a type of pasta that's curly on the edges. Sometimes it is 2 cm (¾ inch) wide, sometimes it is just wide.

Serves 10

PREPARATION TIME: 1 HOUR

COOKING TIME: 20 MINUTES

octopus juice and oil (see page 50)

leftover garlic heads from cooking the octopus

1 kg (2 lb) ripe tomatoes, peeled and seeded, or canned

800 g (1¾ lb) pasta riccia (a curly pasta, sometimes called lasagnetta or large maccheroni)

1 cup grated pecorino

chilli to taste

fresh basil or parsley

After the octopus has been cooked you are left with about 1 L (4 cups) of oil and about the equivalent in octopus juice. There are also half heads of garlic. Squeeze out the garlic flesh and set aside.

Place some of the oil and juice in a pot and add enough tomatoes to thicken the sauce and to dilute its saltiness. Cook on high heat until reduced. If the sauce becomes too salty, add more tomato — it is hard to be precise here. There are too many variables and this is 'make do' food; make do with what you have balancing out the flavours as you go. Persevere and you'll have a terrific sauce and any porous pasta — egg-based or not — will drink up the juices in no time. The leftover oil and juice refrigerate well for several days, and the sauce will also keep a few more days if well refrigerated. The second time around, you can add some seafood, like mussels and prawns.

When the sauce is reduced, cook the pasta in plenty of salted, boiling water until *al dente*. Combine the sauce and pasta in a large pot and let the pasta 'drink up' any residual liquid in the sauce. Add cheese, chilli and fresh basil.

You can fry up some chorizo-style sausage separately, slice and add to the pasta.

SPAGHETTI AL NERO FREDDI CON INSALATA DI PESCE

SQUID-INK PASTA WITH FISH SALAD

Black pasta is pasta that has been coloured with the so-called ink of squid or cuttlefish. The latter is in fact more tasty but harder to get hold of. If you cut open the tube of these creatures, you will find the ink sac. Depending on how the fish has been handled, the sac may be full or broken or almost empty, so look for squid that are as intact as possible. You can buy squid ink from specialist shops if all you want is black pasta.

Black homemade spaghetti look dramatic with any sauce, but the interesting thing is that you can pre-cook them, chill them and then use them as the base for a salad. The sky is the limit here when it comes to possible combinations of flavours — perhaps a salad with yabbies or any other crustacean or a cheaper option with capsicums (bell peppers), fresh tomatoes, basil and extra-virgin olive oil, or anchovies and parsley . . .

Serves 6

PREPARATION TIME: 1½ HOURS

COOKING TIME: LESS THAN 5 MINUTES

PASTA
500 g (1 lb) plain (all-purpose) flour
5 eggs
15 g (½ oz) squid ink

SALAD
1 cup finely julienned raw calamari
light extra-virgin olive oil
juice of 1 lemon
1 tablespoon chopped chilli
fish sauce
12 cooked and shelled yabbies (see page 53)
fresh coriander
extra fish sauce
cucumber strips
skinned and diced tomato

To make the pasta, mix the flour, eggs and squid ink in a large bowl until well combined (wear gloves to avoid dying your fingernails black). Knead until a smooth dough, then form a ball, cover with a damp cloth and allow the dough to rest for a while.

Set up your pasta machine. Cut off a small piece of dough, flatten it with your hands and start pushing it through the first stage or setting of your machine. (If the dough sticks, flour it before putting through the pasta machine.) Put it through several times at the same setting, then go on to the next setting until you reach the last notch of the pasta machine. Pass the pasta through the spaghettini cutter attachment.

To cook, boil the pasta in plenty of salted water and when *al dente* plunge into iced water. Drain and lightly toss in oil before use.

Marinate the calamari in olive oil, lemon juice, chilli and a little fish sauce. Toss with the spaghettini and the yabbies, coriander and extra fish sauce if necessary. Serve with a salad of cucumber strips and tomato.

PASTA FATTA IN CASA

HOMEMADE PASTA

Serves 6

PREPARATION TIME: 30 MINUTES
3 cups plain (all-purpose) flour
5–6 medium-sized eggs

Combine the flour and eggs in a large bowl until well incorporated. I rarely find two batches of pasta to be the same, because of the temperature of the room, because flour is never the same, and because of the variations in egg size. Make sure your dough is not too wet and sticky. If it is, add more flour and knead it in quite vigorously. If it is too dry, add a few drops of water at a time. (Water is a very powerful agent. It takes very little to make the mixture sticky and slippery.) Once you have a smooth dough, keep kneading for several minutes until you are certain that all components are well integrated. Form a ball, cover with a damp cloth and let it rest for a while.

Now set up your pasta machine, giving yourself plenty of space in which to work. Cut off a small piece of dough, flatten it with your hands and start pushing it through the first setting of your machine. Put it through 3–4 times, or until you have a regular shape, which is when your sheet is at least as wide as the rollers. It does not matter if it is a little zigzagged at each end, so long as it is as wide as the rollers all the way. This is not for aesthetic reasons only: a regularly shaped pasta sheet minimises waste, especially when making ravioli.

To achieve a regularly shaped sheet from the start, do not be afraid to fold the first roll on itself and push it through several times. If it appears a bit wet, add more flour. Flouring is important all the way to prevent sticking. Do not stack the sheets of pasta on top of each other. If you have a few and you are distracted from your task, you may return to find them stuck together. Once you are through the first setting of the machine, skip one and go on to the next. There is no need to go through each of the six or seven settings to make good pasta.

Proceed in the same manner until you are close to the last setting. At this point you can stop if you intend to cut fettuccine — for which all machines have an attachment — or pappardelle, large strips that you have to cut by hand, or tagliolini, thin strips that you also have to cut by hand. I prefer the second-last setting as the pasta cuts a little thicker than the last; very thin pasta can turn to glug in the boiling water.

For these three shapes, cut your sheet about 30 cm (12 inches) long. Push through the appropriate machine attachment for fettuccine or cut the pappardelle 1 cm (½ inch) wide. Fold the sheet on itself several times to make cutting easier. If you cut very thin strips — no more than 4 mm (¼ inch) wide — you will obtain tagliolini, which are very good for seafood sauces, tomato-based sauces and soups.

If preparing cannelloni or lasagna, I suggest you proceed all the way to the last setting. These sheets are very delicate and useful for many preparations, including vegetarian lasagna, fish-based or meat lasagna. I love a large, delicate pasta sheet as a wrapper for cannelloni with the traditional filling of ricotta and silverbeet.

If you are cutting pasta for lasagna, stay within 10 cm (4 inches) in length. It will expand further when you cook it. With cannelloni, find a length that suits you, although I prefer them not too long.

Most machines have a spaghetti attachment too; the cut strands look square but round off when cooked. If you like them thin, like angelhair, stay with the second-last setting. If you like them chunky (ideal for a tomato and tuna sauce) take the sheet to the third setting; while it looks too thick, it will go through and produce marvellous spaghetti.

Lasagna and cannelloni pasta sheets require pre-cooking. Do this in plenty of salted water and when still *al dente*, plunge into cold water to cool briefly and lay out on a clean cloth sprinkled with Parmesan to stop sticking. A light béchamel will cover and keep moist cannelloni and lasagna. Sauces that are derived from the light cooking of vegetables in oil can also be poured over the heated dish, but here we may well be going outside the boundaries of home cooking.

These are general guidelines and, at least in cooking, rules are made to be broken.

TAGLIATELLE NERO CON CALAMARI

SQUID-INK PASTA WITH CALAMARI

Squid-ink noodles are now readily available from many shops. If you cannot find them, use penne rigate — short, lined tubes which are readily available in 500g (1 lb) packets. Or you can make your own pasta following the recipe on pages 94–5.

This recipe combines the colour of calamari ink and a rich tomato sauce infused with the flavour of the sea. The calamari must be fresh.

Serves 4, generously

PREPARATION TIME: 1 HOUR

COOKING TIME: 1 HOUR

4 medium-sized calamari

1 onion, chopped

3 cloves garlic, chopped

4 tablespoons or more
extra-virgin olive oil

50 mL (1 ½ fl oz) white wine

2 cups peeled tomatoes

1 small chilli (fresh or dried)

salt and pepper

finely chopped parsley

1 teaspoon grated lemon zest

500 g (1 lb) pasta

Clean the calamari and cut the tubes into rings. Cut the tentacles into smaller pieces if you like.

Fry the onion and garlic in some olive oil until translucent. Add the calamari and wine, and allow the wine to evaporate. Add the tomatoes, chilli, salt and pepper, and cook until the calamari is tender, 30–40 minutes.

Finish with parsley, more oil if needed, and the lemon zest.

Cook the pasta in plenty of salted boiling water until *al dente*. Drain and combine with the sauce. Cheese is optional.

TAGLIARINI FREDDI CON CAPPERI, OLIVE E SALSA DI POMODORO

COLD PASTA WITH CAPERS, OLIVES AND TOMATOES

Tagliarini are not quite as wide as tagliatelle but are not thin like angelhair pasta either. Tagliarini lie somewhere in-between, resembling linguine. This recipe is a little unusual as the sauce is cold, which inevitably causes the pasta to be almost cold when eaten. It is not a winter dish and commercial, egg-based tagliatelle make a more than reasonable substitute.

Serve 6

PREPARATION TIME: 20 MINUTES

COOKING TIME: 20 MINUTES

500 g (1 lb) egg tagliarini
3 tablespoons tomato paste
6 tablespoons extra-virgin-olive oil
2 tablespoons small Italian capers
3 tablespoons chopped black olives
1 clove garlic, finely chopped (optional)
chilli flakes
fresh flat-leaf parsley
freshly grated parmesan

Cook the tagliarini in plenty of salted, boiling water until *al dente*. Drain.

In a bowl, mix together the rest of the ingredients except the cheese.

Toss the pasta into the sauce and sprinkle with cheese.

It is surprising how appealing tomato paste is when eaten in this fashion. Clearly, the better the quality of the paste, the better the result. As a young lad I hitchhiked through Italy almost without a penny. In my backpack I used to keep some crusty bread and a tube of tomato paste. Sometimes I'd live on that and fresh water for up to three days — and I was much leaner, believe me!

CANNELLONI ALL'ITALIANA

CANNELLONI

Cannelloni have gained a bad reputation in Australia on account of the many poorly made versions served up over the years. In part, they are also the victim of food fads that systematically destroy any culinary achievement in Australia.

Cannelloni are easy to make, cheap and versatile. Pre-cooking the pasta sheet for cannelloni may be the off-putting thing. However, if you cool each sheet of cooked pasta in plain water and lay it on a tea-towel sprinkled with grated parmesan cheese as you go, you'll find the sheets easy to handle.

Serves 4

PREPARATION TIME: 2 HOURS
COOKING TIME: 15 MINUTES

PASTA

½ recipe Pasta Fatta in Casa (see pages 94–5)
enough tea-towels sprinkled with parmesan
to prevent the cooked pasta from sticking
125 mL (½ cup) runny cream
olive oil
garlic
1 cup peeled, seeded and diced fresh tomatoes

FILLING

3 oven-baked potatoes (skin on)
1 cup ricotta
½ cup goat's cheese
½ cup grated parmesan
fresh mint or any other herb of choice
salt and pepper

Prepare the pasta according to the instructions on pages 94–5 and roll out. Cut into 12 regular 8 cm (about 3 inches) squares. Bring a large pot of salted water to the boil. Add the pasta sheets, perhaps one at a time until you get the hang of it, and when *al dente*, lift out and place in ice water to refresh. Rest on a dry tea-towel sprinkled with grated parmesan.

Preheat the oven to 180°C (350°F).

To make the filling, peel the potatoes, mash the flesh coarsely and mix with the cheeses, herbs, salt and pepper.

Spoon the filling onto the bottom third of the pasta sheets and roll up into a sausage shape. Place on a lightly buttered baking tray, seam side down, and add the cream. Warm through in the oven for about 15 minutes.

In a frying pan, heat the olive oil, add the garlic and tomatoes. Warm through.

When the cannelloni is ready, spoon over the tomato sauce and divide into 4 portions.

Alternative filling

Leeks are greatly appreciated in Italian and French cooking. For an alternative cannelloni filling for four people slowly stew the chopped white part of four medium-sized leeks. When soft but not mushy, add a cheese of your choice and season to taste with salt and pepper. Roll up in the pasta sheets and bake.

A little melted gorgonzola mixed with a little mascarpone would work well as a sauce.

AGNOLOTTI CON RIPIENO DI CARNE

AGNOLOTTI WITH A FILLING OF BEEF AND VEAL

I do not know what it is that makes me salivate at the thought of agnolotti or any other filled pasta in the ravioli or tortellini family. It may be that these pastas were reserved for the great occasions at my house, although they are standard food in other parts of Italy. Or maybe because this pasta is delicate, tasty and texturally pleasing. The dish also demonstrates that the cook has put some real effort and skill into his or her preparation and thought about the filling and the accompanying sauce.

Filling pasta with meat is an old trick. Often the meat is the finely minced leftovers of the previous day's roast combined with cheese or leftover sauce. I particularly like leftover roasts or braised meats like veal or lamb shank, which are sticky and flavoursome. The sauce from braised meats can be chilled so that the fat rises to the top and can be discarded.

In the Italian language 'agnolotti' refers to something like a half-moon shape, although in Piedmont — where agnolotti are an artform — the square shape we call ravioli is almost acceptable. I prefer the half-moon or crescent shape, and particularly one with the edge sealed using the appropriate tool.

Anything can go into agnolotti, from cheese and vegetables to meat or fish. Here I suggest a filling made of meat cooked in red wine and vegetables with some tender veal mince.

Serves 6

PREPARATION TIME: 45 MINUTES

COOKING TIME: A FEW MINUTES FOR THE AGNOLOTTI

FILLING

400 g (14 oz) beef neck

butter

olive oil

2 cups equal quantities of chopped
onions, celery and carrots

1 small sprig rosemary

500 mL (2 cups) good red wine

200 g (7 oz) veal mince

salt and pepper

1 egg

parmesan

extra egg

extra flour

250 mL (1 cup) sauce from the
beef braising liquid

PASTA

300 g (10 oz) plain (all-purpose) flour

3–4 eggs

Seal the beef neck, preferably in one piece, in a little butter and oil in a saucepan. Add the chopped vegetables, rosemary and red wine. With the lid on, cook the meat and vegetables until the wine has evaporated and the meat is very tender, almost falling apart. If you run out of braising liquid and the pot is drying up, add some beef or chicken stock or hot water. When the meat is cooked, strain the braising liquid and place it in the refrigerator. Cut the meat into small pieces, remove any sinewy parts and place the meat in the food processor together with some of the braised vegetables.

In the meantime, sauté the veal in a frying pan in some oil and butter. Leave it pink, and add to the food processor. Blend the mixture to a paste. Adjust for salt and pepper. Add the egg and cheese and combine to obtain a mixture that's not too wet or too dry.

Prepare a pasta according to the instructions for Pasta Fatta in Casa (see pages 94–5), but using the quantities of flour and egg stipulated here. Roll through the thinnest setting of your machine in as long a strip as you can handle.

Lay out the pasta sheet on a workbench and place the filling at 2 cm (¾ inch) intervals along the top third of the pasta. Brush around the filling with egg and fold over the bottom edge. Press down well to seal the filling. Sprinkle generously with flour. At this point, you may want to cut the agnolotti into squares or cut into half-moon shapes with a round cutter. If you have the implement, crimp the edges.

Cook the pasta in plenty of salted boiling water until they are done. Drain.

To make the sauce, reheat the braising liquid in a saucepan. Stir in a piece of butter to make it glossy and rich. Pour over the pasta and serve.

RAVIOLI DI PICCIONE CON SUGO DI PICCIONE

PIGEON RAVIOLI WITH PIGEON SAUCE

When dealing with pigeon, separate the breast from the rest of the carcass and cook lightly in a frying pan. The carcasses and legs should be cooked slowly to obtain precious braising juices. The meat on the legs, if suitable, can be added to the breast meat and minced together.

Serves 6

PREPARATION TIME: 2 HOURS, LONGER FOR THE STOCK

COOKING TIME: 5 MINUTES

FILLING
1 cup equal quantities of chopped
onions, celery and carrots
olive oil
4 pigeons (8 breasts)
2 sage leaves, chopped
salt and pepper
1 egg
grated parmesan

PASTA
300 g (10 oz) plain (all-purpose) flour
3–4 eggs
1 egg yolk
extra flour

pigeon bones and legs
a splash of red wine
Chicken or Veal Stock (see page 61)
butter
extra grated parmesan

To make the filling, sweat half the chopped vegetables in olive oil in a skillet until they are soft. Chop the breast meat and add to the vegetables. Add the sage, salt and pepper and cook until the meat is pink. Process the mixture to a paste in a blender. Add the egg and enough cheese to obtain a soft but firm paste.

Prepare a pasta according to the instructions for Pasta Fatta in Casa (see page 94–5), but using the quantities of flour and egg stipulated here. Roll through the thinnest setting of your machine. Cut the sheet in half. Place one half aside and on the other, place two lines of filling at regular 2 cm (¾ inch) intervals. Brush some egg yolk on the other pasta sheet and place over the filling, making sure to seal well so that no air pockets form. Sprinkle generously with flour and cut into individual ravioli.

In the meantime, heat a little olive oil in a saucepan and sweat the other half of the vegetables. Add the pigeon bones and legs, brown, then deglaze with a little red wine. After evaporation, add some chicken or veal stock. Reduce and strain through a sieve. Remove the fat and other impurities and reduce the sauce again to a glaze. You can incorporate some butter into the sauce.

Cook the ravioli in plenty of salted, boiling water until done. Drain.

To serve, heat the sauce gently in a large pan. Add the ravioli and some cheese, toss and serve at once.

ROTOLO DI PASTA CON RIPIENO DI CARCIOFI

ROLLED PASTA WITH ARTICHOKES

Homemade pasta rolled into a long log, wrapped in a clean tea-towel and cooked in water has been described in many other cookery books. I'd like to add my version, which contains artichokes instead of spinach or mushroom. Ricotta remains the binding agent, but the nutty flavour of artichokes makes this an interesting variation on a familiar theme.

Serves 6

PREPARATION TIME: 1 HOUR

COOKING TIME: 20 MINUTES IF THE ARTICHOKES ARE ALREADY COOKED

FILLING
about 4 artichokes

lemon juice

olive oil

garlic, chopped

1 bunch parsley

enough Chicken Stock (see page 61) to cover

300 g (10 oz) ricotta

2 eggs

½ cup assorted tender leaves of
young mint, parsley and chives

butter

½ cup grated parmesan

salt and pepper

PASTA
300 g (10 oz) plain (all-purpose) flour

3–4 eggs

To prepare the artichokes, remove the outer leaves, and cut off and discard most of the stem. Peel the remaining stem and cut off about 1 cm (½ inch) of the leaf tips. Drop the cleaned artichokes into water and some lemon juice as you go to prevent discolouration.

Heat olive oil in a pot and gently fry the chopped garlic. Add the artichokes and parsley, and add enough chicken stock to cover. Put a lid on the pot and lower the heat to medium. Cook for about 1 hour or until the artichokes are soft. Cool.

Remove the artichokes from the pot when cold, reserving the braising juices. Discard any remaining hard leaves, and scoop out the choke. Mash the artichokes with the ricotta, eggs and herbs.

Prepare a pasta according to the instructions for Pasta Fatta in Casa (see page 94–5), but using the quantities of flour and egg stipulated here. Roll through the thinnest setting of your machine to make 2 strips 45 cm (18 inches) long. Wet the top edge of one and stick the other on to it to make a wider sheet about 45 cm (18 inches) long. (Or make it to any length you desire; this is just my preferred size.)

Place the pasta sheet on a tea-towel and spread the filling evenly all over. Fold in the ends, and roll up the pasta using the tea-towel to guide you. Tie it securely with string at regular intervals like a salami, but not too hard. Place this pasta 'sausage' in a deep tray full of boiling, salted water and cook for 15–20 minutes on the stove top.

Preheat the oven to 180°C (350°F).

Unroll the rotolo and cut into serving portions. Place in a baking dish and reheat in the oven.

Warm up the artichoke braising juices, add a little butter, cheese, salt and pepper, and stir through. Remove the rotolo from the oven and serve with the sauce.

You can freeze the whole 'sausage' — just roll it in cling wrap and freeze. When you want to cook it, remove the cling wrap and place the frozen rotolo in a tea-towel, tie it up, then place in a pot of boiling water for 45 minutes.

PIATTI DI PESCE

Fish has a mystical aura about it, if you ask me. It is not so much catching it — that surely gives anyone a buzz. I remember catching bay salmon at Philip Island on the surf beach: running in when the swell receded, casting a line out into the white foam with a long rod and running back before the waves had a chance to catch me. Then, settling back on the sand waiting for the top of the rod to bend suddenly and jerk, and grabbing it before it was pulled into the water by one, sometimes two or even three large fish. It isn't much of a fish for eating, so it is best filleted the same day and fried in a light batter. I ate large quantities of salmon like that. Some days I'd catch mullet near the shore, in the shallow water. Mullet is a great-tasting fish cooked there and then in the same manner as above.

There are a lot of underrated fish in Australia. Some of it is very good for fish stock, like gurnard. It is ugly to look at, but very good, especially in a dish called *caciucco*. This truly Tuscan delicacy is often overlooked even though it contains two distinct classic Tuscan elements that have caught people's imagination all over the world — good olive oil and a piece of bruschetta-like bread. Australia is an ideal place for a *caciucco*: we have all the fish and all the crustaceans you'd expect from the Mediterranean Sea.

As a child, I was fascinated by all the fish that was brought into our farmyard by a little smelly man called Checchi. He would rock up into the yard every Tuesday and Friday in his three-wheeled truck with his selection of sparkling creatures. A huge block of ice kept all that silvery fish cool. One day, Checchi, who was always in a hurry, battling as he was against ice-melt, took a left turn into the yard a bit too fast, lost control and ended up with the front wheel in the cow-piss pit. Ironically, a cow is all the power we had to pull him and his truck out of their misery. That day he was smellier than ever.

Checchi's fish came from the fish market, but in my mind that crucial step was always ignored. My thoughts went straight to the trawlers I could see out on the horizon whenever (rarely) I went to our nearest seaside location of Jesolo. Oh, how I envied fishermen!

As I said, there is a lot of good fish in Australia. A fair bit of it is fairy cheap by world standards. It is also available fresh, rather than frozen. Fresh is a definition to be used with extreme care: a trawler stays out at sea for a while with the catch kept very cold. By the time the fish goes to market and is resold through a retail outlet, it is no longer all that fresh. Still, we have little choice in these matters.

There are also many fish preparations. The recent fashion of steaming fish Asian-style is overtaking the old poaching method. A good poached fish, surrounded by the appropriate vegetables and accompanied by a mayonnaise is the marine equivalent of a *bollito misto*. If you know my passion for *bollito*, then you will understand my liking of poached fish. Salmon is the most readily available and has the most meat, making it economical to use. Ask your fishmonger to assist you in the choice of fish for poaching. When I was working to a budget, I must confess that I poached quite a bit of trevally. It was a bit stringy and a little dark, but I got it for only two dollars!

Steamed, poached, pan-fried, deep-fried and oven-baked, whole or filleted, cooked in tomato for pasta sauces, grilled lightly, grilled over an open fire, soused or eaten raw, curried and stewed — the list of ways of preparing fish goes on and on. If you are not taken by fish — and in that I include crustaceans — you are seriously in trouble.

TROTELLE ALLA GRIGLIA
GRILLED TROUT

Remember the late 1970s? The early 1980s? When all trendy restaurants used to serve trout stuffed with scallop or prawn mousseline? Then trout became unfashionable and it was almost smoked out of existence. I reckon that of all farmed fish, trout is still one of the best — cheap and very often fresh. What more can you ask of a fish?

Small trout make great grilling, especially if basted with olive oil.

Serves 4

PREPARATION TIME: 10 MINUTES
COOKING TIME: 10 MINUTES

4 × 200 g (7 oz) small trout, heads on
extra-virgin olive oil
salt and pepper
lemons

Cook the trout on the grill, basting frequently with oil without causing flames. When the fish is cooked — do not overcook it — split in half and remove the bones. They'll come away easily enough.

Dress while warm with olive oil, salt and pepper and a squirt of lemon juice. The skin is tasty if not badly burnt.

SNAPPER AL FORNO

BAKED SNAPPER

There are times of the year when largish snappers are available aplenty. It's a great fish, with a head suitable for a Malaysian curry or to make fish stock for a creamy fish risotto.

The sides of fish that are not too big — up to, say, 2–3 kg (4–6 lb) — are not stringy (a negative quality that is sometimes found in large fish) and are suitable for oven-baking. When I think that a fish that size would cost a fortune in Europe, I am so thrilled to eat it.

Serve 4

PREPARATION TIME: 15 MINUTES
COOKING TIME: 10 MINUTES

100 mL (⅓ cup) extra-virgin olive oil
2 sides snapper with belly bones still in
1 cup peeled and diced tomatoes or
canned tomatoes
12 black olives
a few cloves garlic, peeled
4 thin slices lemon
1 tablespoon dried oregano of the best quality

Preheat the oven to 180°C (350°F).

Pour the olive oil into a baking dish. Place the snapper in the dish, skin side down. Scatter all the other ingredients on top and bake for 10 minutes. If the fish is still opaque, it is likely to not be cooked. If small pearls of white juice are forming on it, it's overcooked, so keep a close watch.

Serve at once on a platter with the juices and the resulting sauce around it. You can add, with moderation, a drizzle of fresh olive oil.

MURRAY COD AL LIMONE, POMODORO E CIPOLLA

MURRAY COD WITH LEMON, TOMATO AND ONIONS

I have written extensively on Murray cod in A Gondola on the Murray, *but here
I come again with another recipe that I have tested and believe is suited to other firm,
white fish fillets. You may think that the slices of lemon used in this recipe are unpalatably
strong. They are not. You will be pleasantly surprised at how well the
flavours come together.*

Serves 4

PREPARATION TIME: 15 MINUTES
COOKING TIME: 8 MINUTES

2 small knobs butter
4 thick slices cod or a firm-fleshed white fish
8 sets of 1 slice onion, 1 slice tomato and
1 slice lemon, 3 mm (^{1}/8 inch) thick
85 mL (^{1}/3 cup) white wine
salt and pepper
85 mL (^{1}/3 cup) cream
2 tablespoons chopped wild fennel or dill or
fennel tops

Place a baking dish over low heat and melt the butter. Add the fish, and with the help of a spatula, assemble the piles of vegetables all around. Add the wine and season lightly with salt and pepper.

Place in an oven preheated to 180°C (350°F). After 5 minutes, pour in the cream and fennel, and continue to cook until ready — 8 minutes should be enough.

WESTWARD WATERS

Watch a small snowmelt
sliding its gloss down a snowgum's trunk

it becomes the Murray,
a ditch draining across an old sea-floor,
falling a man's height in a day's march

a plain whose patterns were immense
gridded to one-mile blocks,
bend after bend, the pure snow-melt
snaking and queuing its way round mallee dunes,
dirtied where a spring of salt wells milkily in
from salt lake buried in the old sea sands

past clear lakes of ribbon grass
that nourish duck and perch
— or turned to mud-swill by the carp;
the river-bends, brown water loop upon loop
swirling or sullenly back-eddying,

under the aging grey-box forests,
a possum meal snoring in each trunk
past the old peppermint alleys
planted when anything foreign was better

past paddocks that try to sweep over dunes
and end in a blown red curl of sand
— sewered, re-filtered, re-returned
to the great red-gum parks, salt swallowers,

passing Willandra's tributary that never delivers,
Mungo with its dry fish-bones
and saltbush like glaucous seaweed waving
translucent in heat-sick air

turning south, south, down

till the warm last of the snow melt dribbles
to the sea near Adelaide.

MARK O'CONNOR

BACCALÀ AL POMODORO

SALT COD WITH TOMATO AND OLIVES

I am so fond of baccalà that I could eat it every day. The important thing is to understand that the water the baccalà is soaked in must be changed constantly for up to three days to eliminate most of the salt. It is best to cook it with potatoes as these will counteract any excess salt. Choose olives that are not too salty and by all means make it chilli-hot if you wish.

If you want to know more about this fish, read Cod *by Mark Kurlansky, and you will appreciate its importance.*

Serves 4

SOAKING TIME: 2–3 DAYS
PREPARATION TIME: 15 MINUTES
COOKING TIME: 30 MINUTES

600 g (1 1/4 lb) baccalà (salted cod)
olive oil
2 cloves garlic, whole
3 cups peeled tomatoes, chopped
1 cup diced potatoes
1/2 cup black Ligurian olives
fresh parsley
125 mL (1/2 cup) extra-virgin olive oil, for serving

You will need to soak the baccalà in cold water for 2–3 days, changing the water frequently.

Heat some olive oil in a pan and add the garlic. When fragrant, remove and discard the garlic cloves. Add the tomato and the potato and cook them until just soft. Break the baccalà into chunks and add to the pan with the olives. Cook until the baccalà is soft. Break parsley over it and add olive oil when you serve, and a little hot chilli if you like.

A GONDOLA ON THE MURRAY

PESCESPADA NELL'OLIO D'OLIVA

SWORDFISH IN OLIVE OIL

Many people reminded me that I did not provide the recipe for swordfish in olive oil in my first book, which appeared on the television program.

It is a very simple recipe that relies on submerging the fish in a bath of good-quality oil heated to no more than 40–50°C (100–120°F). You may have to turn the flame on and off to maintain the heat. The heat on the bottom of the pot is a little stronger than the heat of the oil itself. It is this interplay of temperatures that cooks the fish on the outside only and reasonably quickly.

It is important that the fish be fresh. Even a few hours too old may impart an unattractive odour to fish flesh. There is also a question of what to do with leftover oil. If you chill it, you can reuse it or use it to cook the octopus on page 50. Once again, there is not much point cooking a recipe only once and spending time and money on it: instead, your refrigerator should be a working refrigerator, with food coming from and going into it.

Serves 6

PREPARATION AND COOKING
TIME: 15 MINUTES OR LESS

1 L (4 cups) extra-virgin olive oil, or more
1 head garlic, cut in half across
1 kg (2 lb) swordfish, in one piece

Heat the oil with the garlic in a deep-sided, non-stick heavy-based pot. Test the temperature with your finger — if it gets too hot, turn the heat down or off. Add the fish. Turn the fish around a few times, so that all the sides are in contact with the bottom of the pot, which is hotter.

The fish will take a few minutes to cook evenly on the outside. Remove it from the oil and let it rest. When you cut it, it should be cooked on the outside without flaking and the middle should be pink. I serve it with grilled vegetables and a mayonnaise. It can be served with tossed leaves or a potato salad.

PESCESPADA CON FINOCCHIO

SWORDFISH WITH FENNEL

Fish like swordfish and marlin seem quite widely available these days. I am very fond of them, especially when combined with wild fennel tips. Cut the fish into very thin slices that can be stuffed (secured with a toothpick) and cook gently in a little olive oil either on the stove or in the oven. Either way, cook them only lightly.

Serves 4

PREPARATION TIME: 30 MINUTES

COOKING TIME: 10 MINUTES

12 large slices swordfish, 5 mm (¼ inch) thick or thinner if you like

1 cup breadcrumbs

1 tablespoon lemon juice

1 clove garlic, finely chopped

2 tablespoons grated pecorino

2 tablespoons chopped wild fennel or ordinary fennel tops or dill

4 tablespoons extra-virgin olive oil

salt and pepper

extra olive oil

extra breadcrumbs

extra grated pecorino

Cover the fish with cling wrap and flatten with the side of a heavy knife. This may be necessary if the slices are too narrow.

Mix the breadcrumbs, lemon juice, garlic, cheese, fennel, oil, salt and pepper in a bowl, adding the olive oil gradually. The mixture must be moist but not too oily or too salty.

Place some filling on a slice of fish, roll up and secure with a toothpick. Repeat with the rest of the fish and filling.

Heat a little olive oil in a pan large enough to accommodate all the rolls and cook them gently, turning them over from time to time. Season with a couple of turns of the black pepper grinder. Sprinkle the top with more breadcrumbs and cheese.

Finish cooking in an oven preheated to 180°C (350°F) for a more uniform result. It may take up to 10 minutes, but not much more, as swordfish is best eaten slightly underdone.

WHITING AL VAPORE
STEAMED WHITING WITH LIME LEAVES

Whiting is still available in southern Australia at a reasonable price. It is a delicate fish, perhaps one of the most delicate. Everyone knows about whiting in beer batter, or perhaps grilled. Here I suggest you steam the fish on a plate with a little butter and kaffir lime leaves. Lime leaves are very popular now with the advent of Asian cooking. I even managed to grow a small kaffir lime tree in my garden! I like the lemony scent without the acidity. It is like having an instant, natural perfume at one's disposal. A few leaves are enough to infuse the fish and sauce with the most delicate and fragrant flavour.

For 2 jumbo whiting
PREPARATION TIME: 15 MINUTES
COOKING TIME: 5–10 MINUTES

8 fresh kaffir lime leaves
a knob of salted butter
2 fish, preferably with the bones removed
salt and pepper

Place the lime leaves and butter on a heatproof plate and put the fish on top. Season with salt and pepper. Place the plate in a steamer set over gently boiling water and steam until ready. If the fish is deboned, 5 minutes will suffice. If not, up to 10 minutes may be needed, depending on the size of the fish.

Use the butter and other resulting juices as the sauce and the leaves — if not too grey — for decoration. Lift out the fish with a long spatula, especially if it has been deboned.

WHITING AL POMODORO E CAPPERI
WHITING WITH TOMATO AND CAPERS

Given the availability of whiting, another rewarding way of preparing it is to cook it in a pan with diced fresh tomato, some small capers and a little white wine. Like all Italian cooking, this dish is good only if the ingredients are good. If the fish is old, the tomato green, the olives nondescript and the capers too salty you will get a very unsatisfactory result.

This dish is best finished in the oven. In this instance — and in the preceding one — it may be better, if you feel brave enough, to remove the fish bones while leaving the fish intact. That is very simple if you have a good, sharp, small boning knife. Place the fish on a chopping board and run the knife along the back of the fish and do the same on the other side. Ease as many bones out as you can and remove the rest with tweezers. Leave the tail and the head attached to each fillet. Snap the bone or cut it with scissors. The fish will look like a sandwich and your diners will be pleasantly surprised to find a whole fish free of bones.

For 2 jumbo whiting
PREPARATION TIME: 20 MINUTES
COOKING TIME: 8 MINUTES

2 tablespoons extra-virgin olive oil
$^{1}/_{2}$ cup diced fresh tomato
1 teaspoon finely chopped garlic
2 large whiting
a splash of white wine
1 tablespoon small salted capers
10 small black olives
fresh basil leaves or flat-leaf parsley

Preheat the oven to 180°C (350°F).

Heat a pan large enough to accommodate the fish and suitable for going into the oven. Add the olive oil, which should be instantly hot. Add the tomato, then the garlic and fish. After a minute, carefully turn the fish over so that you don't bruise or damage it in any way. Add a splash of white wine, the capers, olives and herbs.

Place the dish in the oven. If you have boned out the fish, the cooking time is very short, about 6 minutes. If the fish is left whole and is largish, 10 minutes may be necessary.

Use a long fish lifter to remove the fish from the pan. Make sure the sauce does not dry out.

CALAMARI RIPIENI IN UMIDO

STUFFED AND BRAISED CALAMARI

Calamari, the most sought-after members of the squid family, are also, unfortunately, the victims of overexposure, particularly in Italian restaurants, where they come inevitably deep-fried. More recent Asian recipes have broadened the appeal of calamari: I really like them steamed with ginger and garlic in the Chinese fashion.

Stuffed calamari are fiddly, but they have three distinct adavantages: they can be prepared beforehand and reheated; they can be served as an entrée or main course; and they accompany pasta, rice or polenta equally well. Stuffed calamari can be red-cooked with tomato or white-cooked without tomato, but the latter doesn't give you much sauce to play with. For all these reasons, and their good taste, stuffed calamari are worth persevering with.

Serves 4

PREPARATION TIME: 1 HOUR
COOKING TIME: 45 MINUTES

8 calamari, with tubes no longer than 12 cm (4³/4 inches)
1 cup equal quantities of chopped onions, celery and carrots
extra-virgin olive oil
3 cloves garlic
125 mL (¹/2 cup) white wine
1 cup breadcrumbs
¹/2 cup grated pecorino
2 eggs
1 cup chopped flat-leaf parsley
salt and pepper
2 cups canned tomatoes, chopped
extra flat-leaf parsley, chopped

Pull the head from the calamari and set aside. Pull off the wings. Empty the tube — you'll find that you can reverse it like a glove. Keep the ink sac if you wish — it can be frozen to make squid ink pasta (see page 93). Peel the skin off. Cut the tentacles from the head and do not let the eyes spray you. Cut the cartilage from the wings.

Sauté the chopped vegetables in a little olive oil with the garlic. Add the wings and tentacles and cook for a few minutes. Add the wine and let it evaporate. Take off the heat. When cool, process in a food processor to a coarse paste. In a bowl, mix the paste with breadcrumbs, cheese, eggs, parsley and salt and pepper.

Stuff this mixture into the calamari tubes and secure the ends with a toothpick.

Heat some olive oil in a pan and add the tomatoes. (You can drop a little grated lemon or orange zest in the tomatoes for a special perfume.) Sauté until the tomatoes are soft, then add the stuffed tubes and cook for 30 minutes or more on a low heat or until all the flavours are well integrated. Add a little water, chicken or fish stock if the sauce dries up. Sprinkle more parsley over the top and serve.

LE CARNI

Meat was food that my family could not readily afford. A visit to the butcher's shop was a trip of certain importance because there you had to pay with real money. Once a year, Dad would buy some guts and some beef to stretch the quantity of available pork meat for salame-making. That was a grand occasion, but there weren't many like that. Mind you, it hadn't always been that miserable. I had an uncle who was a *mediatore* — a broker, whose job was to buy and sell animals. Unfortunately he died prematurely when I was a child, and a certain amount of meat went with him to another world. Anyway, occasionally Dad would buy a calf's head. It had some good meat attached to it, and made excellent stock. He'd sit the head on the bike's handlebars and pedal 3 kilometres to our home. In those days it was not unusual to see people carry all manner of things on the handlebars: chooks, fish, cows' heads, children, parcels etc.

Poultry and pork featured more frequently on our table than beef, which is usual in most peasant cultures. Pork came to the table in a preserved form, whereas poultry went straight into the pot. If there were something from a cow, it would have been the lesser cuts. That's how the great braised or boiled dishes were developed, mostly using the cheaper cuts. In gastronomy, though, I think that a good treatment of the lesser parts elevates them to the same culinary distinction as the more sought-after cuts.

In Australia, however, things were always different. This country relied for a long time on beef and lamb, so here all types of meat have been generally cheaper than in other countries. Meat and three veg became the standard meal, both in the home and at the restaurant.

When the cultural gastronomic elite(s) got the work, however, particularly in the last twenty years, they declared this food daggy, boring and non-sexy. The elite(s) embraced French–Mediterranean, East–West, and some dumbed-down Asian at the exclusion of indigenous produce (and please, let's not argue on the meaning of the word indigenous), which was seen as unhealthy or boring. It is true that the early diet relied too much on meat, but by embracing something else so uncritically, and with such gusto for putting down all things Australian, they threw out the baby, the water, the bath and the whole house. Try to serve a porterhouse! Goodness, they'd think you were a hopeless cook stuck in another era.

I have written about this before. Australians throw away everything at the drop of a hat. Who drops the hat? A plethora of food writers like myself, opinion-makers, journalists (more specifically), imported books and videos and cooking shows looking for something to do. There is never a moment in the day when we are not tortured by a new ingredient we are told we must have. And the result? We are cooking fewer and fewer meals at home.

While I am an unresolved meat-eater, and I don't appreciate huge reds, I'd like to propose a menu consisting of a big Aussie red, a porterhouse cooked as you like it, and a good Australian-made brandy. The pinot brigade will say your palate is sick, the health freaks and trend-setters will say you are daggy, outmoded and hopeless, and that you will die of cancer, and the cops will be out there to remind you that you are a bloody idiot! Sound like John Laws? Maybe, but I am not him. I come from a totally different set of opinions: I just hate the way Australians hate themselves. And through food, you see the picture very clearly.

But back to meat. Once again, I have looked mostly for things you can do with an Italian accent.

LA PORCHETTA DI SASKIA
SASKIA BEER'S PIGLET

*One of the most old-fashioned, romantic ideas about a banquet is the notion of
roasted piglet. When I cook one (often supplied by Saskia Beer), I do it in a porchetta style, the
classic Italian way of first removing all the bones (leaving the head intact) and stuffing it with
sausage and chicken meat. I like porchetta because it can be eaten cold — it tastes even better
the day after — and it goes a long way if you have a party with many people to feed.*

Serves many!

PREPARATION TIME: 1 HOUR

COOKING TIME: 2 HOURS OR UNDER

1 kg (2 lb) Italian sausage meat

500 g (1 lb) chicken breast, minced

1 cup equal quantities of chopped onions,
celery and carrots, cooked until soft
in a little butter

2 cups breadcrumbs

1 cup grated parmesan

5 eggs

10 sage leaves, chopped

5 cloves garlic, finely chopped

salt and cracked black pepper

1 female piglet, 5–7 kg (10–14 lb)

white vinegar or lemon juice

olive oil

Preheat the oven to 200°C (375°F).

In a bowl thoroughly mix the sausage meat, chicken mince, vegetables, breadcrumbs, parmesan, eggs, sage, garlic, salt and pepper. Cook a little of the mixture to see that it holds and is properly seasoned. (You don't want the stuffing to fall apart when you cut the piglet.) If the stuffing falls apart, add more eggs, cheese and breadcrumbs and test again.

Place the piglet legs up on a large chopping board. Burn off any hair. Rub the skin with a little vinegar.. Cut through the legs and remove the bones. Separate the ribs from the meat and go all the way up to the front legs. Cut through again and follow the meat around the neck.

Place the stuffing in the cavity and close it neatly. A metal skewer may be helpful to keep the belly tightly closed. Tie it up with string, as you would with any meat roll, and place on a rack over a baking tray. Rub with oil and sprinkle with salt. You can bend the piglet to make it fit your oven.

Cook for 20 minutes or until a nice colour begins to show. Lower the temperature to 180°C (350°F) and keep going for the next 90 minutes or less — depending on size — turning at least once. Make sure it is cooked around the neck area, which is the thickest part. The pork can be eaten cold and keeps well in the refrigerator, although a loss of skin crispness will be inevitable.

MAIALE ARROSTO CON FINOCCHIO

ROAST PORK WITH FENNEL

When I prepared a roasted loin of pork on the rib for the second series of Gondola, *the film crew polished up the finished dish in moments. To me that was proof that when pork is good, it can be exceptional. That particular loin came from a friend who cares more about making the point about good pork than being identified. If you look hard enough you'll find him or others with the same passion. Only attempt this dish when you can get good pork. If the pork is too lean, for instance, it will be dry. If you cop an old boy, it will be smelly.*

Serves 6

PREPARATION TIME: 10 MINUTES

COOKING TIME: 1 HOUR 30 MINUTES

4 bulbs fennel, cut into large pieces
4 medium-sized carrots, cut into large pieces
2 onions, quartered
several cloves of garlic
a loin of pork, on the rib, 2–3 kg (4–6 lb)
a little olive oil
salt

Preheat the oven to 180°C (350°F).

Place the fennel, carrots, onions and garlic in a baking dish and put the loin on top. Rub the olive oil all over the loin and rub a little salt on the skin. Place in the oven and roast for about 90 minutes or until the meat is done to your liking. Skim off any excess fat from the baking dish as you go. Check to make sure nothing gets burnt. Remove the loin and keep warm.

Place the vegetables on a platter and keep warm. Discard the fat on the bottom of the dish, keeping only the brown juices (a little goes a long way). You don't really need to serve a gravy with this dish, but if you like, add a little beef stock to stretch it.

The vegetables, particularly the fennel, can be eaten with the pork. Otherwise, serve with salad, roasted potatoes with garlic and fresh pan-tossed spinach.

COLLO DI AGNELLO

BRAISED LAMB NECK

Lamb, Australia's great resource, possesses a profound appeal for me because it was non-existent in my family's diet. Mind you, many other Italians had lamb, a regional speciality in many parts of the Peninsula, but we didn't.

Serves 6

PREPARATION TIME: 20 MINUTES

COOKING TIME: 90 MINUTES OR MORE

3 lamb necks, split in half lengthwise and sinew removed

plain (all-purpose) flour

olive oil

1 cup equal quantities of chopped onions, celery and carrots

3 cloves garlic, whole

125 mL (½ cup) red wine

2 cups crushed tomatoes

1 L (4 cups) Lamb or Beef Stock (see page 61), fairly concentrated

Preheat the oven to 180°C (350°F).

Wash the necks well and remove any impurities. Dry them and toss them in a little flour. Shake off any excess, leaving only the lightest of coatings.

Heat some olive oil in a pan and seal the necks all over. Set aside.

In a baking dish, fry the vegetables and garlic in some oil. Add the necks — bone side down — and add the red wine. Let it evaporate. Add the tomatoes and stock. Cover the top with greased paper and foil.

Bake in the oven for a good 90 minutes. At that point, the meat should come off the bone. If not, cook it for longer, perhaps adding more stock. Remove the meat from the bone and set aside. Push the cooking liquid through a sieve and chill. The fat will come to the top. Discard the fat, heat the sauce and place the neck meat in it to warm up.

Accompany the dish with Pea Custard (see page 130) or mashed potatoes.

CREMA DI PISELLI

PEA CUSTARD

Mashed potatoes or polenta are typical accompaniments to a braised dish or anything with a richly flavoured sauce. An alternative and slightly more elegant way of accompanying the lamb neck on page 129 is to serve it alongside a custard of peas.

Serves 8

PREPARATION TIME: 20 MINUTES

COOKING TIME: 25 MINUTES

olive oil
250 g (8 oz) peas
500 mL (2 cups) cream
6 eggs
salt and pepper

Heat a little olive oil and add the peas. Gently sauté them, add the cream and cook until soft. Blend the mixture until smooth, then add the eggs and salt and pepper. Pour into 100 mL dariole moulds and place in a baking tray filled with water to come halfway up the sides of the moulds. Bake in an oven preheated to 120°C (250°F) for 25 minutes, or until set.

We had shepherds coming down from the mountains during the winter months to feed their mobs on the dry grass along the roads. Sometimes the sheep would be allowed into a property to eat whatever was available. None of us ever thought to ask for a lamb in exchange for money or anything else. That is how closed we were in our world, and how closed the shepherds were in theirs. People from the same country, separated by a few days of walking, would not talk to each other and remained firmly engaged in their own thing. To be honest, we looked at them with a mixture of curiosity, compassion and disdain, as if we, who didn't even have toilets in our houses, were better off. I am now convinced that the shepherds, who came down from beautiful valleys of the Dolomites and the mythological world of cymbric culture, looked at us with equal disdain.

Once, early in the spring, a mob ventured into a paddock of tender, green wheat and ate the lot. The mayhem that followed was unpleasant, something I do not want to keep in my memory. The wheat grew stronger afterwards, as if it had had a hair cut, but there was no way of calming our neighbour when the event took place. Suspicion of people from other cultures leads to stupidity and irrational behaviour, often triggered by the pretext of something inconsequential.

SPALLA DI AGNELLO IN UMIDO
SLOW-BRAISED SHOULDER OF LAMB

I can understand people who do not want to fuss over a neck of lamb, but find it unpardonable when they ignore a shoulder of lamb. Some of the people I have worked with would rather perish under my cleaver than do something about the many shoulders of lamb we had — and have — as a consequence of buying the whole carcass. Deboning it is very easy. The morsels of meat from the shoulder can be cooked slowly in a rich tomato and vegetable base to become a main course or a pasta sauce.

Serves 8

PREPARATION TIME: 30 MINUTES
COOKING TIME: 2 HOURS

2 cups equal quantities of chopped onions, celery and carrots

3 cloves garlic

olive oil

1 kg (2 lb) shoulder meat, roughly cubed

a little red wine

salt and pepper

2 cups cubed potatoes

500 g (1 lb) tomatoes, skinned, seeded and chopped

a few rosemary leaves or thyme

water or stock

Sweat the chopped vegetables and the garlic in some olive oil. Add the meat, stir and cook it a little, then add the wine and let it evaporate. Let the juices ooze out of the meat and the sauce reduce. Season with a little salt and pepper and add the potatoes, tomatoes and herbs.

Cook over a low heat for a long time, adding some water or stock if the casserole dries up a little. It is ready when the oil comes to the top, a bit like when you cook a curry. That may take up to 2 hours and in that time the potatoes may have disintegrated. That's fine, because they add creaminess to the dish.

The same dish makes a great sauce for homemade pasta.

NIGHT OF THE GOAT

Kid is young goat. Known as *capretto*, it is best used when weighing in at 6–7 kilograms. I have included a recipe for goat's blood out of deference for the culture of people who live around me and who have taught me a lot about this animal.

When Maggie Beer rang to tell me that she was going to attend the Mildura Writers' Festival, we agreed that I would cook kid for her so she could look at different parts of the animal. She also told me that Stephanie Alexander would be coming as well. I don't know about you, but the thought of cooking for these two formidable women virtually paralysed me. But, as we say, the show must go on.

I planned to have the dinner at my house. That was the most discreet way of escaping from other friends who would also be looking for a place to eat after a late festival reading.

First I paid a visit to Uncle Tony Senior. He promised me the kid and to have it delivered to Auntie Cathy's place, where the cooking would take place under her direct supervision. Auntie Cathy is very particular about cooking. I washed and scrubbed the split kid's head at least eight times before she deemed it fit for cooking. I had to remove every bit of hair from the meat and so on. I was reminded of how meticulous these women are, and how much of an intrinsic part of their art that is.

I returned to the festival with the understanding that Auntie would deliver the cooked goat at my place by 9 p.m. All she had to do, after all, was to cook it for one hour or until tender. She had a better oven and a better-equipped kitchen.

I asked my guests to be at my place at 10 p.m., and to bring along the writer and our friend in common Peter Goldsworthy; another writer, my friend Shane Maloney; and Irish poet

Mathew Sweeney, a brilliant man we had kidnapped from the Adelaide Writers' Festival.

I left the festival on my motorcycle, planning in my mind to set up the table, place the champagne on ice, turn on the air-conditioner — it was a stinking hot night — when I ran out of petrol at the bottom of the hill on the way home. I had forgotten that I had switched on the reserve lever a few days earlier. So I determined to push the vehicle some 700 metres home up the hill. I got there exhausted, sweating profusely. I thought all was well until I realised that the house key that was supposed to be on my key ring was missing. The only key left on the ring was the one stuck on the motorcycle ignition — everything else had somehow fallen off.

Then I lifted the doormat to retrieve the spare key I had given Auntie to let herself into the house. 'Put it back,' I had said, 'that's our spare key.' It wasn't there.

With mounting panic, I tried to force open all windows and doors, but the house was impenetrable. And the guests were about to arrive.

I resolved to go to Auntie's house back down at the bottom of the hill to get the key. To get there quickly, I thought I'd take the old bike, the one that I use on television. It had a flat front tyre, but I thought it was fine to go downhill. In the dark I bumped into something and fell.

At Auntie's place, all the lights were on and one or two of a dozen cars usually in the yard were there. Encouraging signs, but my pants had caught in the bike chain. The bike uses the pedals as brakes, so you cannot reverse them to get the pants out. The only way to free the pants is to actually take them off, lift the bike, push the pedals with your hands to a full revolution and they come out at the other end. No, I said to myself, I am not wasting time, let alone taking the risk of being found by a sudden visitor in the act of taking off my pants. (A similar incident occurred when filming *Gondola*. I think the ABC has that tape.) So I pulled hard, cursed the bike and lost a pair of Henry Bucks cotton pants.

I knocked on the doors, yelled and screamed, but the house was empty.

Back on the old bike, torn trousers, and up the hill. I could not bear the thought of pushing another vehicle uphill again, so I hid the bike in the scrub. (I treasure the bike and did not want it stolen. I also had visions of my director, Chris McCullogh, saying, 'How are we going to film without the bike?')

Back at the house, in a bath of sweat, I cursed myself for not keeping a mobile phone on me, and waited for my guests. The only way now was to tell them some of the truth and drive back to town, seek my wife out of the wedding she was running at the hotel, and get another house key.

Finally the guests arrived and that is what we did. At the hotel, I found my other uncle, Tony Junior, Auntie Cathy's husband, laughing with Mario, my brother-in-law. One glance at me was enough. He said, 'Sorry, sorry, I have your key in my pocket . . . you see, our oven broke down, so now auntie is in the hotel's kitchen cooking your kid . . .'

I went ahead to accomplish what I had intended to do an hour earlier. At home, everyone helped to set up and prepare the salad and appetisers. The cooked goat duly arrived with a profusion of apologies from Auntie and all was well. Except the air-conditioner, which had been left on for too long on too low, decided to freeze up, putting it out of action for many hours.

Dinner was consumed in Moroccan conditions, but we all had a good time.

And that's what happened on that hot Mildura Night of the Goat.

VERZATA CON COSTOLETTE DI MAIALE E SALSICCE

CABBAGE WITH PORK RIBS AND PORK SAUSAGES

Savoy cabbage is used a lot in Italian cooking, for soups, risotto, and with pork. The verzata *is a classic dish of cabbage, pork ribs and skins from Lombardy, where the cold winters invite diners to steamy, hot dishes that please the senses and fill the stomach.*

This festival of calories loves a slightly acidic red wine that cuts through the dish without killing its flavour. Arnie Pizzini and his cousin Fred have caused a minor revolution by introducing Italian wine varieties to the King Valley. Marzemino is a Northern Italian variety that Arnie has successfully grown, and his 1998 Marzemino is an ideal complement.

Pork ribs and Savoy cabbage are easily found anywhere. For pork sausages, tell your butcher that you want minced pork shoulder mixed with 3 g of black pepper and 26 g of salt per kg. Any respectable butcher will do it. Ask for mince with a little fat, or the sausages will be too dry. And remember that the butcher does not need to tie the sausage at regular intervals: it can just be a long coil. You cut off 5 cm (2 inch) pieces for the verzata *and refrigerate or freeze the remainder.*

Good delis have continental sausages in stock. Look out for any made by Jonathan's of Melbourne. Like me, Gianni and his family have migrated from Treviso and they know a good sausage.

Serves 6

PREPARATION TIME: 20 MINUTES
COOKING TIME: 1 HOUR OR MORE

6 small pieces pork skin
a little olive oil or butter
600 g (1 1/4 lb) pork ribs
salt and pepper
2 medium-sized Savoy cabbages, thinly sliced
leftover small pieces of parmesan crust (optional)
6 pork sausages

Blanch the pork skins in hot water for 1 minute.

Heat a little oil or butter, add the ribs and skin, season a little with salt and pepper, and add the cabbage. It will reduce in volumn very quickly. If the mixture is too dry, add some water or stock. Add the parmesan crusts and cook until the cabbage has become really soft and the meat is almost coming off the ribs.

Fry the sausages in a pan until half-cooked, then add them to the *verzata* to finish cooking with the cabbage. If you put them in from the start, they get too tough for my taste, so add them at the last minute. Serve hot on fine, soft mashed potatoes.

You can also add some diced Asiago cheese or another cheese that is full of flavour and not too hard.

SCORTECHINO DI FILETTO

EYE FILLET SLICES

*When you need something quick and easy — excuse the cliché — thin slices of eye
fillet cooked only on one side are very good. You can also use venison in a similar fashion.*

*This simple meat dish is perfect with a salad of rocket and some roasted potatoes.
For the potatotes, peel and cut them into 2 cm × 1 cm (¾ inch × ½ inch) pieces and drop them
in a pot of boiling water for a few minutes. Drain well, then place in a roasting tray
with more rosemary, salt and whole unpeeled garlic cloves. Add sufficient
olive oil to roast until golden, turning once or twice.*

Serves 4

COOKING TIME: 2–3 MINUTES

4 tablespoons olive oil
12 slices best eye fillet, 5 mm (¼ inch) thick
1 tablespoon rosemary leaves
salt and pepper
a few drops of best-quality balsamic vinegar

Pour a little oil into a very hot pan. Cook the beef six slices at a time without turning until small droplets of blood appear on top of the slices. Scatter the rosemary over the pan. When you think the fillet is done on one side, add some salt, pepper and a few drops of the best balsamic vinegar. Each batch should only take a few moments to cook.

BRASATO DI CODA DI BUE

BRAISED OXTAIL IN RED WINE

Another fabulous Australian resource is oxtail. I do not know if it is popular in Australian households or not, but I hope it is, because it is cheap and tasty. Deft cooks in the 1980s used to turn oxtail into a baroque dish by deboning and stuffing it with a tasty filling. I have tried it and succeeded several times, but it takes an inordinate amount of time to execute.

The thought of a tender, juicy dark dish of braised oxtail on the bone is enough to make me salivate. The procedure for cooking tail is much the same as for lamb neck, although you can cook tail in a pot on the stove top. By adding some strong beef stock, this dish easily becomes a dark, flavoursome soup. I have served it with small ravioli, in the form the Italians would call guazzetto.

Oxtail, cut into regular pieces, is best kept in cold water and a pinch of salt for 5 hours. After that it should be placed in a pot with water, a little onion, celery, carrot, parsley and thyme and gently brought to the boil for a few minutes to eliminate impurities. Discard the water and place the tail pieces on a dry cloth.

Serves 4

PREPARATION TIME: 30 MINUTES
COOKING TIME: UP TO 3 HOURS

2 cups equal quantities of chopped onions, celery and carrots

olive oil

2 oxtails, cut into regular pieces

250 mL (1 cup) red wine

2 L (8 cups) Beef Stock (see page 61)

2 cups of peeled, seeded and chopped tomatoes

a little bunch of thyme and parsley

Preheat the oven to 180°C (350°F).

In an oven tray or casserole or similar (on the stove top) sweat the chopped vegetables in a little olive oil. Add the tail pieces (including the little ones at the end — they are good for flavour) and the wine. Allow the wine to evaporate, add the stock, tomatoes and herbs.

Cover the top with greaseproof paper and foil. Place in the oven and cook the tail until the meat falls off the bone — up to 3 hours. Halfway through, ensure there is enough liquid to last the distance or add more.

When ready, remove the best pieces and set aside. Pass the sauce through a sieve and chill. The fat will come to the top. All this can be done ahead.

Remove the fat, put the sauce back in a suitable pot, melt it gently and add the oxtail pieces to warm through. I find the flavour of grated orange most agreeable with oxtail, so I suggest an orange gremolata.

To make orange gremolata, grate an orange, avoiding the pith. Chop some parsley and mix with the grated zest. Some people add a little chopped garlic to the gremolata. I don't.

PORTAFOGLI DI VITELLINO AL PARMIGIANO

POCKETS OF VEAL WITH PARMESAN

Tender loin of veal is used to make scaloppine, another abused dish that I confess to liking a lot. In an effort to reinvent scaloppine of veal with an ingredient I also like a lot — Parmigiano Reggiano — I thought of making some pockets of veal and Parmigiano. The technique is very easy. After bashing out some veal (the butcher can do that for you) put one slice on a work surface, place some shavings of parmesan on it, perhaps with a leaf of fresh sage, place another slice of veal over that and seal the edges with some water. Lightly flour the pockets and proceed as if you were cooking scaloppine. The melted cheese will cause explosions of flavour in your mouth, which I think you will like a lot.

Serves 4

PREPARATION TIME: 40 MINUTES

COOKING TIME: 10 MINUTES

24 thin slices veal
12 sage leaves
parmesan shavings
plain (all-purpose) flour
olive oil
butter
white wine or Chicken Stock (see page 61)
salt and pepper
a dash of cream

Place 12 slices of veal on a work surface. Place a sage leaf on each and sufficient cheese (not much is needed) for the filling. Wet the edges with a little water and top with another slice of veal. With a mallet or the handle of a knife hit the edges slightly so that they will hold together.

Gently flour these 'pockets' and fry them in a little oil and butter. Toss out any excess fat, deglaze with white wine or chicken stock, season and add a little cream just to bring the sauce together. With such a large number of 'pockets' you may have to use two frying pans and work fast. These delicate veal dishes don't like waiting.

Serve with puréed spinach.

PICCATINA AL LIMONE

VEAL WITH LEMON

The most tender part of the veal is the loin, sometimes called strap. The veal round is also good, but a little troublesome to cut evenly. Piccatina is a slice of veal almost like scaloppine, but is not flattened as much. Ask your butcher to allow a thickness of under 1 cm (½ inch).

Veal is so adaptable to many flavours, from dry to sweet wines, citrus, mushrooms, herbs and so on. Lemon is a natural partner for veal. Veal is cooked quickly to retain its juices, but at the same time be careful to avoid it 'bleeding' on the plate. This often happens when instead of searing the meat, it is kind of 'stewed' for a short time.

Serves 4

PREPARATION TIME: 10 MINUTES

COOKING TIME: 5 MINUTES

2 tablespoons butter
2 tablespoons olive oil
a little plain (all-purpose) flour
12 slices veal, under 1 cm (½ inch) thick
salt and pepper
125 mL (½ cup) Chicken or Veal Stock
(see page 61)
juice of ½ lemon

Heat the butter and oil in a pan. Lightly flour the veal slices, shaking off any excess. Place neatly in the pan and fry both sides until the meat is cooked and does not bleed. Season with salt and pepper.

Remove the meat from the pan and transfer to serving plates. Add the stock to the pan, reduce and add a little lemon juice. Pour the sauce over the veal and serve at once.

POLLETTO ALLA GRIGLIA CON AGLIO E ROSMARINO

GRILLED CHICKEN WITH GARLIC AND ROSEMARY

This is one of my favourite dishes of all times: a young, tender chicken, grilled on a real fire after being marinated with fragrant herbs, olive oil and lemon juice. I suggest a chicken of just over 1 kg (2 lb) for best results, so you may have to grill two if you need more. Glenloth chickens from the heart of the Mallee are fantastic, as are those from Kangaroo Island and the Barossa Valley. I am not seeking their favour when I say that these producers — and there may be many more out there — are responsible for making chicken respectable again. My gratitude to them is infinite and each week I await the delivery of these chooks with the same sense of expectation as I did the first time. I reckon there should be a kind of award nomination system for chickens: best flavour, best tenderness, best texture, and an overall winner.

Serves 4

PREPARATION TIME: 10 MINUTES (EXCLUDING MARINATING)

COOKING TIME: 10-15 MINUTES

1 × 1.2 kg (2½ lb) chicken
125 mL (½ cup) olive oil
juice of 1 lemon
mixed herbs, such as rosemary and thyme
3 cloves garlic, crushed
1 teaspoon salt

Split the chicken along the backbone and flatten. Marinate with all the other ingredients for 3–4 hours or overnight in the refrigerator.

Carefully grill the chicken over an open fire, making sure it does not burn. Serve slightly pink on the bone. In the absence of an open fire, use a grill: one of those ridged ones that sit on top of the stove. In this case, wrap a brick with foil and place it over the chicken, skin down first, until it browns. Repeat the operation on the other side. It may splutter, but the result is great.

PEPERONI E PATATE IN PADELLA

FRIED CAPSICUM AND POTATOES

This vegetable dish is an ideal accompaniment to the grilled chicken on the previous page.
It is a very simple dish that takes on a special flavour in combination with good
extra-virgin olive oil and garlic.

Serves 4

PREPARATION TIME: 10 MINUTES
COOKING TIME: 15 MINUTES

3 large red or green capsicum (bell peppers)
or both
3 large potatoes
85 mL ($^{1}/_{3}$ cup) extra-virgin olive oil
2 cloves garlic, whole
salt
a few sprigs herbs (optional)

Cut the capsicum into 1 cm ($^{1}/_{2}$ inch) strips after removing the seeds and membranes. Thinly slice the potatoes — no precision required.

Pour the oil into a largish non-stick frying pan. When the oil is hot, add all the other ingredients and let them caramelise lightly on one side. Turn over from time to time to avoid burning.

The vegetables should be cooked in 10–15 minutes. Some sliced potato will break down, while some capsicum strips will be darker than others. Squeeze the garlic out of its skin and mix in. This dish is delicious cold and even better over slices of homemade bread.

PETTO DI POLLO AL POMODORO FRESCO

CHICKEN BREAST WITH FRESH TOMATO

*Chicken is the ultimate saviour when it comes to meals. Perhaps even too much so.
The point is that too often, it is dry and unappealing because it is cooked for too long, and often
the quality of battery chicken is not so good. This recipe is a simple stir-fry that relies on fresh
herbs, good extra-virgin olive oil and ripe Roma tomatoes.*

Serves 4

PREPARATION TIME: 15 MINUTES
COOKING TIME: 8 MINUTES

4 chicken breasts, each cut into
4–5 chunky pieces
85 mL (¹/₃ cup) olive oil
1 cup peeled, seeded and diced
Roma tomatoes
2 cloves garlic, chopped
basil leaves
salt and black pepper

Combine all the ingredients in a bowl, mix well and
marinate for 2 hours.

Heat a non-stick skillet and start to cook the chicken
fast on high heat. There should be still enough oil
attached to the chicken; if not, add a little to the pan.
When the chicken is done — after 4–5 minutes — add
all the other ingredients, including any residual oil.
If your skillet is not big enough, divide the mixture
and fry in two lots. If basil is not available, try oregano,
rosemary or coriander.

POLLO AL FORNO CON PATATE
BAKED CHICKEN WITH POTATOES

This dish was shown in Gondola on the Murray, *and took the fancy of many viewers. I have been asked many times to supply the recipe. It is really the simplest way to cook chicken — there is nothing to it. Come to think about it, it is a formula that can be successfully used to cook lamb or goat.*

Serves 4

PREPARATION TIME: 20 MINUTES
COOKING TIME: 40 MINUTES

1 × 1.5 kg (3 lb) chicken
5 potatoes, cut into wedges
125 mL (¹/₂ cup) olive oil
¹/₂ cup grated pecorino
¹/₂ cup breadcrumbs
2 cups peeled, seeded and chopped tomato
2 tablespoons dried oregano of
the best quality
5 cloves garlic
salt and pepper
250 mL (1 cup) water
125 mL (¹/₂ cup) white wine

Preheat the oven to 180°C (350°F).

Cut the chicken into pieces of equal size and place in a baking dish. Distribute the potato wedges here and there snugly, wherever they fit. Pour the oil all over. Sprinkle cheese and breadcrumbs all over, followed by tomato, oregano, garlic, salt and pepper. Finally pour in the water and wine gently, in one place so that it seeps under the chicken pieces. Cover with foil and bake for about 35 minutes. Remove the foil to brown all over until cooked.

FARAONA DELLA BAROSSA

BAROSSA GUINEA FOWL

Guinea fowl is a little different from what the Italians call farmyard birds. They are elegant without being ostentatious. If I were to compare them to the world of fashion, I'd imagine guinea fowl to be elegant like French fashion. Then, I may be wrong in these matters.

My mum had 50 to 60 of these birds at any time. So did our immediate neighbours. One of them, Gnagna Erminia, who was of Yugoslav origin and was said to look wildly beautiful when young, had children who had a butcher's shop in town. According to a persistent rumour, many birds found their way there. Hence each of my mother's fowls had a wing clipped; our immediate neighbour, Gnagna Vittoria, clipped something off the feet; and the third lot were left alone. The birds were thus identified and mischief could not take place.

*I remember guinea fowl as dark meat. Mum roasted it in the fashion of the time —
too much — and served it with a sauce made of liver, capers and anchovies.
I have tried unsuccessfully to re-create the sauce.*

Guinea fowls from Saskia Beer's Barossa farm seem a little different in appearance from how I remember them, but they are unquestionably good. The trick is to cook them quickly, in two separate stages, in a very hot oven. I separate the breast from the leg and thigh first and seal this 'maryland' in a hot pan and pop that in the oven to cook to a pink stage. I let that rest for 10–15 minutes. In another pan I sear the breasts and, depending on the thickness, I may finish the cooking in the oven. The meat must remain very pink.

I think the trick with all these birds is to cook them quickly, to pink, to retain juices and flavour, or to pot-roast them with other condiments. (Unfortunately, many people think that cooking pink is a sin and cannot bring themselves to like rare meat.) Game like guinea fowl and pigeon have to be 'hung' for a while to tenderise the meat.

Serve 4

PREPARATION TIME: 10 MINUTES
COOKING TIME: 30 MINUTES

2 guinea fowl
$1/2$ cup lard, chopped to a paste with
4 tablespoons rosemary
4 tablespoons olive oil

Preheat the oven to 200°C (375°F).

Remove the breasts and the 'maryland' from the guinea fowl. You can roll back the thigh meat by removing the bone — you'll be left only with the drumstick bone. Spread the lard over the skin evenly.

Heat some oil in a pan, seal the legs and pop them in the oven for 10 minutes. Remove and let the meat rest.

In another frying pan, seal the breasts in some olive oil.

To serve, slice the breasts and put them next to the roasted leg.

If you wish to go the whole way, chop up the carcasses and brown in some oil with garlic, thyme, a little carrot, onion and celery. Add 1 L (4 cups) chicken stock, and cook until well reduced. Strain the sauce, skimming and adjusting the seasoning as necessary, and serve with the bird.

SANGUE DI CAPRETTO ALLA CIPOLLA GIALLA

BLOOD PUDDING WITH ONIONS

Blood pudding is not everyone's favourite, but it is understood and not frowned upon. So I do not want you to be repelled by the idea of eating goat's blood. Now, I know that you are not going to do it, and even if you wanted to, it would be pretty difficult to execute this dish. Usually dishes that are difficult are not included in my books — I hope you have noted the near absence of truffles, crayfish, marron and many, many other ingredients that are simply too exotic or expensive or even unreliable to feature here!

The reason for including this recipe is twofold: it shows how far inventiveness goes in using every component of an animal and I want it recorded to honour the people on my wife's side who have taught me a lot about food. When their generation passes away, no-one will know about sangue di capretto.

As the animal is slaughtered, the blood is collected in a bowl and immediately taken to the kitchen where a pot of boiling water is at the ready. The blood is poured into the water and allowed to simmer for about 20 minutes, while impurities are removed. The blood turns into semi-solid blocks that are removed from the water and allowed to cool. Then they are ready to be sliced and fried. Looking at it, you'd think it's a block of chocolate!

Serves 4

PREPARATION TIME: 20 MINUTES

COOKING TIME: 10 MINUTES

300 mL (10 fl oz) solid blood
2 onions, sliced
4 tablespoons olive oil or more as required
2 bay leaves
salt and black pepper
a pinch of dried chilli flakes

Slice the blood as you would slice liver — thinly. Sweat the onions in the oil with the bay leaves until they are translucent and soft. Push them to one side of the frying pan and add the blood. Season with salt and pepper and turn over. (Unfortunately, the brown chocolate colour will turn a dull grey.) Sprinkle with chilli flakes. One minute of cooking on each side is ample. Serve at once.

SANGUE DOLCE

Blood is used not only as a savoury component in Italian cooking, but also combined with sweet preparations. Visiting my aunt in her fairly isolated mountain village, I was offered a sweet pudding. Her mischievous grin made me suspicious. My interest was further provoked upon presentation of the dish *budino di cioccolato* (chocolate pudding). I played along, for I suspected its origin straightaway, this sweet made with blood that I had read about and heard my grandparents speak of. I also wanted to include my brother and sister in the game. Admittedly, my curiosity was sincere; I wanted to get an understanding of the evolution of the dish due to the restricted availability of produce in these remote villages.

In times past, horses and donkeys were the only means of transport, communities were isolated and the supply of food limited. The altitude made it difficult to grow an extensive variety of fruit and vegetables. During summer, women worked in earnest to preserve all types of food. Cellars were well stocked with whatever could be grown — fruit, vegetables and dairy products in their natural state or having undergone some preserving technique. Any animal that was slaughtered was prepared for long-term consumption to minimise waste, including the blood, which made its way into a number of dishes.

You may be aware of a heavily spiced fruit cake, similar to the panforte of Siena. This cake was typically bound with blood — a shortage of eggs required a substitute protein, and blood was available.

By the way, a small sample of the pudding was sufficient to quell my curiosity. I still smirk at the memory of my siblings' reactions when they found out what they had eaten! **LS**

DOLCI

You will notice a slight change in format in the ingredients in this chapter of the book — they are accurately measured. General cooking is more forgiving compared to cake and pastry-making, where the balance of ingredients and application of technique determine consistent outcomes. You may recall how your mother, an aunt or friend consistently baked cakes, pies or made dessert without accurately measuring. I can see only too well my aunt taking her mixing bowl and filling it to a certain level with flour, cracking in three eggs, adding one small glass of alcohol and another of orange juice. Then the addition of orange zest and three spoons of butter, all quite haphazardly. After working these ingredients to form a dough, she would knead, adding 'just enough flour' to achieve her desired consistency. Typically, this was seldom necessary, as she always used the same measuring implements. This recipe was generously shared around, yet its replication rarely came close to the original.

My point is this — indeed, her measurements were accurate. She always used the same bowl, glass and spoons because these were her standards of measurement, and her intuitive touch always worked the dough to the correct consistency. In my typical 'disciplined' manner, I arrived one day with scales and a measuring jug and worked alongside, weighing the ingredients accurately as she went. The flour was in the vicinity of 550 g (18 oz) to 3 eggs; the butter was almost 50 g (1½ oz), the alcohol and orange juice both around 70 mL

(2½ fl oz) each. Subsequently, her recipe for *crostoli* is included in this book for others to reproduce successfully (see page 166).

Mastering baking can be a little tricky, so please don't deviate from the recipe or alter quantities on your first attempt. Your perseverance will be rewarded with delicious results and, with continued practice, I can guarantee memories of flavours, tastes and textures that will transport you to the Old Country in no time at all. (See also 'A Note about Some Ingredients' on pages 198–200.) **LS**

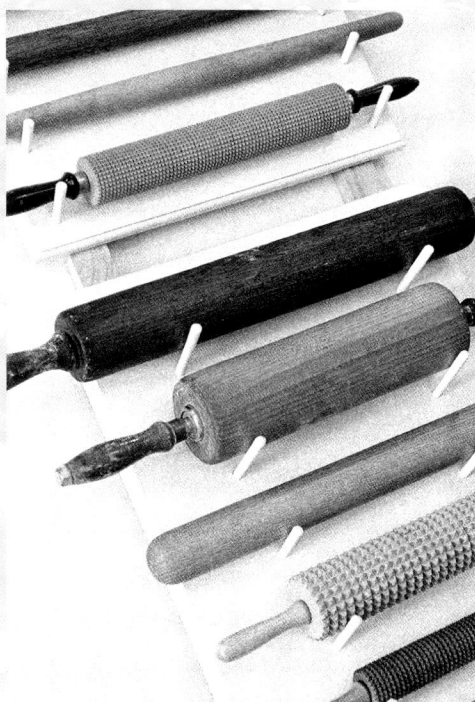

PASTA SFOGLIA

CLASSIC PUFF PASTRY

The Italian name for puff pastry often leaves folks tongue-tied, but for me the French name is difficult to master. Regardless, the term implies a light flaky pastry that results from enveloping the butter in a base dough, then carefully rolling and folding it. This requires a little patience but the rewards are worth it!

Makes 1.25 kg (2 ¹/₂ lb)

500 g (1 lb) unsalted butter, divided into an 80 g (2 ¹/₂ oz) piece and a 420 g (14 oz) piece
500 g (1 lb) plain (all-purpose) flour
a pinch of salt
200 mL (7 fl oz) water

In a large bowl, rub the smaller piece of butter into the flour. (Keep the remaining butter cold.) Add the salt. Blend the flour and water together by pouring the water in a thin stream and mixing slowly so that it acts as a binder. You may do this by hand or in an electric mixer fitted with a dough hook. When the pastry is lightly mixed together, remove to a board and knead with the heel of your hand. Wrap in plastic and rest for 2 hours (or overnight) to allow the elasticity to settle.

Roll dough into a rectangle approximately 28 × 20 cm (11 × 8 inches). Remove the remaining butter from the refrigerator, and beat with a rolling pin into a small rectangle of about 2 cm (3/4 inch) thickness. Place the butter in the centre of the dough and fold in the edges to envelop the butter completely.

Roll the pastry into a rectangle measuring 50 cm × 20 cm (20 × 8 inches). Take care to apply the pressure evenly and not to squeeze butter from the mixture. Keep the ends as square as possible. Fold the pastry into thirds by folding it towards you to a central point, and then back over itself. Grip the rectangle firmly and turn it around 90 degrees so the folds are now right–left in front of you. Now roll it out in front of you again. This rolling technique has now worked the pastry in a different direction. Fold again in three, and you have completed two 'turns'. Cover the well-floured pastry with cling wrap or greaseproof paper, tucking in the ends so they don't dehydrate, and rest in the refrigerator for 1 hour and at room temperature for 1 hour.

Complete two more turns, rest again, and then make two more turns.

A 'six-turn' pastry is a completed pastry. It may be used immediately or stored in the refrigerator, well-wrapped, for up to 2 days. It will freeze, but is better frozen at four turns, so the two final turns are completed after thawing. This will result in the removal of any dry pieces of dough. Remember never to disturb the layers when thawing or rolling.

PASTA FROLLA
SWEET SHORTCRUST PASTRY

Pasta frolla is universally known in some form or another as sweet shortcrust pastry. The following recipe is well known and adapts itself to a multitude of outcomes. The Italians are particularly adept with its use as biscuits, pasticcini *(small dry or filled goods to accompany coffee or spumante for a festive occasion) or as the base for tarts and individual sweet items. The technique differs from the traditional 'rub in' method to incorporate the butter; instead, the butter is creamed with sugar and eggs, then flour is added to finish the dough. The pastry must be chilled before use as freshly made, it resembles a paste.*

Makes 650 g (1½ lb)

200 g (7 oz) unsalted butter
100 g (3½ oz) castor (superfine) sugar
1 egg (optional)
300 g (10 oz) plain (all-purpose) flour

Cream the butter and sugar until the mixture is a pale yellow. Add the egg, if using, then fold in the flour, mixing until absorbed. Or, add the flour to the creamed base and pulse until combined. Do not overmix. The pastry is soft and paste-like at this stage and requires chilling before use.

To use the dough, remove the pastry from the refrigerator, cut or break into pieces and apply some pressure to soften. Lightly knead this softened, cool dough and roll out on a lightly floured bench. Roll the pastry from top to bottom and side to side to extend. (This will ensure even shrinkage when baked.) Use the pastry as directed in each recipe.

CREMA PASTICCERA

EGG CUSTARD

'La bella crema' — no soul has survived a trip to an Italian cake shop without consuming this cream in one form or another. This vanilla custard cream is filled into cannoli, piped into bigne (choux puffs) and lavished into sponge cakes. Once made, it must be chilled to set, then beaten to develop its distinctive velvety-smooth properties.

Makes 700 g (3 cups)

500 mL (2 cups) milk
100 g (3¹/₂ oz) castor (superfine) sugar
1 vanilla bean, split and scraped
3 egg yolks
50 g (1¹/₂ oz) cornflour (cornstarch)

Bring the milk, 50 g (1¹/₂ oz) sugar and the vanilla bean to the boil in a heavy-based saucepan over a medium heat.

Meanwhile, whisk the yolks and remaining sugar together, then gradually fold in the cornflour to form a pale yellow paste.

Carefully pour small amounts of boiled milk onto the yolk mixture, whisking to incorporate. Continue until you have used approximately half the milk with the yolk mixture. Return the remaining milk to the heat and bring back to the boil. Remove the vanilla bean and carefully whisk in the yolk mixture. (At this point you must work fast and carefully as the mass will form quickly.) Continue mixing the thickened cream until it returns to the boil. Transfer to a clean, dry bowl and cover the surface with cling wrap. Chill until required.

To use the cream once it has been chilled, beat until smooth. An electric beater gives a much smoother result than beating by hand.

PAN DI SPAGNA

PLAIN SPONGE

Makes 1 × 26 cm (10½ inch) cake or 2 × 20 cm (8 inch) cakes

5 eggs
100 g (3½ oz) plain (all-purpose) flour, sifted
50 g (1½ oz) cornflour (cornstarch), sifted
100 g (3½ oz) castor (superfine) sugar

Preheat the oven to 180°C (350°F). Butter and flour a 26 cm (10½ inch) tin.

Separate the eggs. Combine the sifted flours.

In a mixer, whisk the egg whites to soft peaks stage and gradually add the sugar. Continue mixing until you have a shiny firm meringue. Reduce the speed to medium and add the yolks one by one, mixing until combined. Remove from the mixer and gently fold through the flours. Stir only until the flours are absorbed.

Pour into the prepared tin and bake for 35 minutes. Or you can use 2 × 20 cm (8 inch) tins, in which case bake for 20 minutes.

PASTA DI MANDORLA
ALMOND MARZIPAN DOUGH BASE

Made according to tradition, and fortunately my first employer, Otterino Pace, instructed me accordingly. Traditionally, blanched almonds are combined with sugar and citrus peel, then passed through a grinder made of stone cylinders, graduating from coarse down to fine. The paste is used as the base for a multitude of biscuits — Ricciarelli di Siena (see page 163), Bocconcini di Mandorla (see page 162) and Crostata di Mandorle (see page 175).

Makes 400 g (14 oz)

80 g (3 oz) candied orange peel
60 g (2 oz) pure icing (confectioner's) sugar, sifted
125 g (4 oz) castor (superfine) sugar
125 g (4 oz) blanched almond meal

In a food processor, pulse together the candied peel and icing sugar. Add the castor sugar and finally the almond meal, mixing all ingredients until a soft, moist ball forms. Wrap in cling wrap if not using at once, and refrigerate until required.

SCIROPPO DI ZUCCHERO
LIGHT SUGAR SYRUP

Makes 400 mL (14 fl oz)

150 g (5 oz) castor (superfine) sugar
350 mL (11½ fl oz) water

Combine the sugar and water and bring to the boil. Cool. Store in an air-tight jar or container in the refrigerator until required.

RICOTTA

RICOTTA CHEESE

*Ricotta is easily obtained these days, however, the recipe is included to encourage you
to make your own as it is extremely simple to do. You'll need to use full-fat milk. I learnt to
make my own when living at Yulara (Uluru, Ayer's Rock), where I worked as executive
pastry chef. Perishable ingredients were very difficult to obtain, given that supplies arrived by
semitrailer twice a week, and the chef did not consider fresh cheeses a priority. Being the
greedy young thing that I was back then, I longed to eat a good cheesecake
and had to resort to making my own cheese.*

Makes 500 g (1 lb) cheese

3 drops lemon juice
3 L (12 cups) milk (4% fat)
250 ml (1 cup) plain yoghurt

Add lemon juice to the milk and leave in a cool place
(not the refrigerator) for 36 hours.

Add yoghurt to the milk, stir to combine, then bring
to boiling point and boil for 1 minute. At this stage the
milk will separate into curds (the fat) and whey (water).
Strain through a cloth or very fine sieve. Discard the
whey and refrigerate the curds that have collected in
the cloth. Use within 3–4 days.

A CHEESY PROPOSAL

I too use ricotta a lot. When I was living in Melbourne a bunch of Sicilian friends and I used to go out to a cheese factory in Thomastown to eat warm ricotta as it came out of the manufacturer's tubs. (I think you can still do it.) You can certainly go and buy a range of products from Italian cheese factories on a Sunday morning. Take the children and show them.

Ricotta is sold in slabs from large blocks. This is rather dry, which is perfect for pastas and cakes. In smaller, 500 g (1 lb) tubs, it is often quite 'wet', especially when fresh. This ricotta is good by itself, either savoury, with the addition of oil and other condiments, or sweet, with sugar, as my children are fond of eating.

Salted ricotta is very salty to my taste. Be careful when using it. Smoked ricotta I have not yet seen in Australia. In the south of Italy, where my wife's father comes from, fresh ricotta is made from ewe's milk. When I tasted it, I thought it was a triumph, especially as a ravioli stuffing. I also noticed that it was perfect with a wine called Aglianico, which goes to show how certain combinations have existed for some centuries without changing.

After one outing to the ricotta factory in Thomastown, I took some of this cheese to my future wife, who lived in a nice flat in the Melbourne suburb of Carlton. I had not yet exposed her to these eccentric outings because I had no idea of what a foodie she would be. All I knew then was that I wanted to marry her without further ado. I put to her my wish, nonchalantly, while eating some ricotta from a small tub. She was sitting on a chair on the balcony of her flat. As the reply was not coming fast enough for me, I prompted her by pouring the contents of the ricotta tub on her head and walked out.

'I want an answer by this evening,' I said.

That is a form of propositioning that I strongly recommend for partners in doubt — it is bound to get a response one way or another! **SdP**

BISCOTTI

BISCUITS

It's the nature of Italian people to always have something to offer when guests drop by — hospitality is the rule, not the exception. So it comes as no surprise that even on a day when the cupboard seems bare, a biscuit can be rustled up from a jar somewhere. Biscuits take many forms in Italy, from simple, almost crude dough rusks to dense, nutty and moist jewels. The recipes included are not difficult to achieve, and provide a variety that will keep everyone happy.

BISCOTTI DI PINOLI

PINENUT BISCUITS

Here is a quick and easy biscuit using pasta frolla. *If pinenuts aren't your favourites, substitute with lightly roasted and roughly chopped hazelnuts or almonds.*

Makes 40

100 g (3 ½ oz) pinenuts, lightly roasted
½ recipe Pasta Frolla (see page 152)

Mix the pinenuts through the pastry and roll into 2.5–3 cm (1–1¼ inch) diameter 'sausages'. Chill.

Preheat the oven to 180°C (350°F). Line a baking tray with non-stick baking paper.

Cut the chilled dough into 4–5 mm (¼ inch) thick slices. Place on the baking sheet and bake for 10–12 minutes, until golden brown. They become firm and crisp as they cool down.

BACI DI DAMA

LADY'S KISSES

*While we 'Aussies' enjoy yoyos as a biscuit, the Italians, who manage to twist
everything into a romantic ideal, call their equivalent lady's kisses.
These more-ish mouthfuls are guaranteed to delight!*

Makes 20 pairs

115 g (4 oz) blanched almond meal
100 g (3½ oz) unsalted butter, softened
115 g (4 oz) castor (superfine) sugar
100 g (3½ oz) plain (all-purpose) flour
100 g (3½ oz) chocolate

Spread the almond meal onto a baking tray, and roast
for 8 minutes in an oven preheated to 160°C (325°F)
until a pale golden colour.

Mix the softened butter with the sugar and almond
meal until combined. Add the flour and fold in until
thoroughly dispersed.

Wrap the dough in cling wrap and chill until firm.

Preheat the oven to 190°C (375°F). Line a baking tray
with non-stick baking paper.

Roll the chilled dough into balls 1.5–2 cm
(½–¾ inch) in diameter. Place on the lined baking
tray (allow a little room for the biscuits to spread) and
bake for 10–12 minutes. The biscuits should be a light
golden colour, and become firm and crisp as they
cool down.

Chop the chocolate into small pieces and melt over
a bain-marie or in the microwave on a defrost setting.

When the biscuits are cold, sandwich with the
melted chocolate.

BISCOTTI DI MANDORLA

ALMOND BISCUITS

These are not the traditional almond biscuits that grace tables on festive occasions but made on a pasta frolla *base. However, they are delicious. Whether made as 'mouthfuls' or as a larger tea biscuit, they are guaranteed to impress.*

Makes approximately 40 biscuits

½ recipe Pasta Frolla (see page 152)
100 g (3½ oz) egg whites
100 g (3½ oz) castor (superfine) sugar
100 g (3½ oz) almond meal
flaked almonds, lightly roasted
icing (confectioner's) sugar

Roll out the Pasta Frolla to 4 mm (¼ inch) thickness, and trim the piece to a uniform square or rectangle. This is easily achieved on a floured, inverted baking tray. Chill.

Make a paste with the egg whites, sugar and almond meal. Spread it finely over the chilled pastry base using an off-set spatula. Sprinkle flaked almonds over the surface and press in lightly. Dust with icing sugar.

Preheat the oven to 180°C (350°F). Line a baking tray with non-stick baking paper.

Cut the pastry into 4 cm (1½ inch) wide ribbons and then cut those strips into 2 cm (¾ inch) pieces. Transfer the biscuits to the baking tray.

Bake for 15 minutes. The biscuits should be a light golden colour, and become firm and crisp as they cool down.

Back: Crostoli; (page 166)
Front: (clockwise from top) Baci di Dama (page 159),
Bocconcini di Mandorla (page 162), Biscotti di Mandorla (page 160),
and Ricciarelli di Siena (page 163)

BOCCONCINI DI MANDORLA

LITTLE ALMOND BITES

Made from the base recipe of marzipan dough, these crunchy little 'mouthfuls' with moist, smooth centres tend to be too easy to eat. Practise caution, or before you know it, the bowl will be empty!

Makes 25–30

1 recipe Almond Marzipan Dough Base (see page 155)
icing (confectioner's) sugar
2 egg whites
150–250 g (5–8 oz) flaked almonds, lightly roasted

Prepare the marzipan dough according to the recipe on page 155. Divide into three pieces.

On a bench dusted with icing sugar, roll the pieces into lengths of 1.5 cm (2/3 inch) thickness. Cut into 1 cm (1/2 inch) pieces and roll into small balls. Dip the balls into egg white and roll into the flaked almonds, pressing slightly so the nuts will adhere. Transfer to a baking tray lined with non-stick baking paper. Allow the biscuits to stand overnight at room temperature so the surface forms a fine crust.

The following day, dust the biscuits with extra icing sugar and bake in an oven preheated to 180°C (350°F) for 10 minutes.

Cool, and store in an air-tight container.

RICCIARELLI DI SIENA
DIAMOND-SHAPED ALMOND BISCUITS

Most Italian cities usually promote a specific dish, cake or product that becomes the definitive local product, so many folk would be aware of the Panforte di Siena, a dense cake of candied fruits and spices. There is another 'classic' from the same town that is lesser known and much easier to reproduce. These almond biscuits have a distinctive shape, and are baked onto edible rice paper. The firm outer shell gives way to a moist almond filling.

Makes 20 biscuits

1 recipe Almond Marzipan Dough Base
(see page 154)
icing (confectioner's) sugar to dust
edible rice paper

Prepare the marzipan dough according to the instructions on page 155 and divide it into 3 pieces.

On a bench dusted with icing sugar, roll the pieces into widths of 1.5 cm (3/4 inch) thickness. Press the rolls flat, so that they are approximately 1 cm (1/2 inch) thick. Cut on the diagonal, re-roll the end pieces and repeat.

Transfer to a baking tray lined with non-stick baking paper and then covered with a layer of rice paper. Allow the biscuits to stand overnight at room temperature. The following day, dust the diamond-shaped biscuits with icing sugar and bake at 180°C (350°F) for 15 minutes.

When cold, store in an air-tight container.

ZALETTI

POLENTA BISCUITS

It will come as no surprise that these biscuits are typically from the north, particularly the Veneto, where goods are commonly enhanced with semolina or polenta flour. Rustic in style and more-ish, they are enjoyed by young and old alike.

Makes 25–30

120 g (4 oz) unsalted butter
90 g (3 oz) castor (superfine) sugar
1 egg
150 g (5 oz) plain (all-purpose) flour
120 g (4 oz) fine yellow semolina
2 tablespoons polenta (cornmeal)
1 teaspoon baking powder
90 g (3 oz) sultanas, soaked in brandy

Cream the butter and sugar in a mixing bowl until pale. Add the egg.

Sift together the flour, semolina, polenta and baking powder. Fold the flours into the butter base with the drained sultanas. Wrap the dough in cling film and chill before use.

Preheat the oven to 180°C (350°F). Grease or line a baking tray with non-stick baking paper.

To shape the biscuits, lightly knead the chilled dough and roll into long 'sausages' 2–2.5 cm (¾–1 inch) in diameter. Cut into 2 cm (¾ inch) pieces and transfer to the baking tray. Press the dough into the trays — these biscuits are not uniform in shape.

Bake for 15 minutes. Cool and store in an air-tight container.

BISCOTTI DI PRATO

PRATO BISCUITS

The term biscotti *seems to apply itself to oversized, very hard, heavy, dry biscuits in Australia. This shouldn't be the case. Once you have tried this, you will have different expectations of what the generic term should imply. These crunchy, light and flavoursome biscuits from Prato, near Florence, are best made in larger quantities because once you start, you simply can't stop. I have deliberately left out the step where these are made as long logs, baked and then sliced — the method here is less tedious and you can eat them sooner!*

Makes 30–40

1 egg
1 egg yolk
125 g (4 oz) castor (superfine) sugar
150 g (5 oz) self-raising flour, sifted
50 g (1 1/2 oz) almonds, roasted
and roughly chopped
1/2 teaspoon anise seeds
3/4 tablespoon olive oil

Preheat the oven to 170°C (330°F). Line a baking tray with non-stick baking paper.

Whisk together the egg, yolk and sugar until thick and pale.

Combine the flour, almonds and anise seeds.

Add the oil to the eggs. Add the flour mixture to the eggs and stir until a sticky dough forms. Roll into pencil-shaped lengths. The dough is quite sticky so dust the workbench well with flour.

Place the lengths on the baking tray, allowing space in between for the biscuits to expand. Bake for 15 minutes until golden. Cool, and store in an air-tight container.

FRIED PASTRIES

Fried pastries are another issue that stirs up national debate in Italy. From the north to south of the country, you'll find various fried sweet pastry items. The north, in particular, are fiercely regional in this area, with minute variations that can be seen from province to province, let alone region to region. Naturally, everyone will tell you in earnest that their mother or grandmother makes 'the very best'!

CROSTOLI
ITALIAN FRIED PASTRIES

The fried pastry strips that are eaten before Carnival are the pride of the cook who makes them. Variations abound not only in shape and degree of thickness, but also with the preferred sweetener, be it castor sugar, icing sugar or honey. Different regions in Italy have different crostoli shapes. Don't be overwhelmed by the quantity of pastry this mixture yields — they are feather-light to eat, and few people can resist them!

MAKES UP TO 60 PIECES, DEPENDING ON HOW YOU CUT THE PASTRY

1 teaspoon baking powder
375 g (12 oz) plain (all-purpose) flour
2 tablespoons castor (superfine) sugar
2 tablespoons unsalted butter
juice of 1/2 orange
zest of 2 oranges
2 tablespoons brandy or grappa
2 eggs
plain flour for dusting
vegetable oil for frying
castor (superfine) sugar

Mix the baking powder with the flour and sugar on the workbench. Rub in the butter. Make a well in the centre of the flour and pour in the juice, zest, brandy and eggs. Slowly bring the flour into the centre, mixing to incorporate. Continue until a dough is formed. Knead well for at least 5 minutes, wrap in cling wrap and rest for an hour. If the kitchen is cool, do not refrigerate.

Divide the dough into three or four pieces. They can be rolled by hand, though I find it easier to use a pasta machine. Working one piece of dough at a time, press the dough in flour and pass it through the machine at the widest setting. Dust with flour again, fold in half and pass it through. (If the dough is sticky, you may have to dust well with flour.) Repeat with the other pieces of dough.

If the dough is awkward to handle, cut into manageable lengths. Ensure all the pieces are rolled through at the first thickness. Continue passing the dough through on each of the subsequent thicknesses until you get to the second last. By this stage you will have several very long sheets of dough of approximately 1.5 mm (1½ inch) thickness. Cut in half if you like to make them easier to handle.

To form individual pastries, the quickest way is to simply cut 3–4 cm (1½ inch) strips across the width. Or, for more decorative pastries, cut into fine strips that can be tied into knots or bows.

To cook the pastries, heat the oil in a deep pan to approximately 175°C (350°F). Use a scrap of dough to test the heat — the dough should become golden in about 30 seconds. Cook the pastries, two or three at a time depending on the size of your pan. Once the pastry is golden and puffed up, turn it over to cook the other side. Remove from the oil and drain on kitchen paper. Sprinkle immediately with castor sugar or sifted icing sugar.

'CICERATA' DELLA NONNA
GRANDMOTHER'S GOSSIP

Nonna's gossip was originally a simple and rather poor dessert that used basic ingredients combined with a little creativity to produce an inspiring wreath of sweetness. (Perhaps the wreath signifies the gossip aspect — what goes around, comes around.) It is essentially a farmhouse dessert with a base of flour and water, though better times have seen the addition of fragrant alcohol and a garnish of candied fruit. In the photograph I have garnished with spun sugar for a nice variation which, although attractive, is a bit time-consuming to do at home.

Makes 1 × 28 cm (11 inch) cake

500 g (1 lb) plain (all-purpose) flour
3 eggs
4–5 drops citrus oil, or orange or lemon zest
1 1/2 teaspoons baking powder
50 g (1 1/2 oz) castor (superfine) sugar
fortified wine, Strega or liqueur
of your choice
vegetable oil for frying
375 g (12 oz) honey
candied fruit (optional)

Combine the flour, eggs, citrus oil, baking powder, sugar and sufficient wine or liqueur to form a firm dough. Lightly knead. Wrap the dough in cling film and rest for at least 1 hour.

Divide the dough into four pieces and roll into long thin sausages of approximately 1 cm (1/2 inch) thickness, then cut into small pieces approximately 1 cm (1/2 inch) long. Roll them into balls.

Heat the vegetable oil in a pan and fry the dough in batches until golden brown. Drain on kitchen paper.

Once all the pastry has been fried, heat the honey in a saucepan large enough to accommodate all the pastry balls. Allow the honey to boil for 3–4 minutes to slightly evaporate, then add the pastry balls and toss to coat well. Remove the honey-coated pastries with a slotted spoon and transfer directly onto a serving plate in the shape of a wreath.

Do not refrigerate this cake as the honey will dissolve. Eat and store at room temperature.

CANNOLI SICILIANI
SICILIAN RICOTTA-FILLED PASTRIES

While cannoli can be found all over Italy these days, the Sicilian variety is distinctive due to the ricotta filling. It is not unusual to find the smooth creamy filling studded with candied fruits, chocolate chips and, occasionally, roasted chopped almonds. Traditionally, the filling has diced zuccata (candied pumpkin), candied orange peel and bitter chocolate chips, and the garnish is a strip of candied orange peel on the surface linking the two fillings — this is said to aid digestion. A fine sprinkle of ground pistachio graces each end.

A pasta machine is easiest for rolling out this dough, but a rolling pin does the job perfectly — it just takes more time and patience. Orange or lemon oil can be purchased from specialist grocers and some continental grocers.

Makes 25

PASTRY
25 g (3/4 oz) castor (superfine) sugar
300 g (10 oz) plain (all-purpose) flour
1 teaspoon baking powder
1 egg
1 egg yolk
1 tablespoon orange juice
zest of 1 orange
1 1/2 tablespoons brandy or grappa
1 1/2 tablespoons olive oil
vegetable oil for frying

FILLING
500 g (1 lb) fresh ricotta
80 g (2 1/2 oz) castor (superfine) sugar
2–4 drops orange or lemon oil,
  or orange or lemon zest
100 g (3 1/2 oz) dark chocolate, chopped
100 g (3 1/2 oz) roasted almonds, chopped
100 g (3 1/2 oz) candied orange peel, diced

Combine the sugar, flour and baking powder in a bowl. Add the egg (reserve the white for eggwash), egg yolk, orange juice, zest, brandy and oil, and mix well. Turn out and knead for 4–5 minutes to form a smooth dough. Wrap in cling wrap and rest for 1–2 hours before rolling out.

If you're using a pasta machine, divide the dough into three pieces, press flat and dust with flour. Feed the dough through the widest setting of the machine several times, each time dusting with flour and folding the dough in half to feed it through again. If your dough is sticky or too moist, dust with flour to absorb the moisture, allowing the dough to come through more easily. (Sometimes the dough tears and looks rough when it comes through; this generally means it is still too damp or you have forced in too much dough.)

Continue until the pieces of dough have been fed through, then set down the machine by one notch and feed the dough through again. (It is important to keep your pieces of dough in rolling order, and go back to the first piece each time you change the setting on the machine.) Continue passing the sheets of dough through until you reach the second-last setting. Pass through once at this width and rest the sheets on the bench.

If you're using a rolling pin, divide the dough into six pieces. Roll each piece out to approximately 5 mm (⅛ inch) thickness and rest. Take the first piece and roll out until the dough is 2 mm (¹/₁₀ inch) thick, and repeat with the rest.

Using a round pastry cutter, cut out a disc of pastry that will wrap around a metal or wooden cannoli rod and overlap by 1–1.5 cm (½–¾ inch). Re-roll all the scraps and continue cutting until all the dough has been used. Make sure that the pastry discs are dusted with flour and stacked on top of each other to stop them drying out.

Grease the cannoli rods lightly with oil to prevent the dough sticking when it cooks. Wrap a disc of pastry loosely around the cannoli rod. Make an eggwash by beating the reserved egg white, and use to lightly brush where the pastry overlaps and press to seal. Continue wrapping the dough discs around the rods until they are all used.

Heat the oil in a deep pan. The oil should be deep enough to engulf the entire pastry. Test the oil with a scrap of pastry — the pastry should turn golden brown and float to the top, and the temperature register 175–180°C (350°F). Cook the cannoli, three or four at a time, depending on the size of the pan.

When the cannoli are cooked, remove and drain on kitchen paper. Carefully remove the rods while still warm. If you have to re-use the rods allow them to cool before re-wrapping with the dough discs (metal rods cool faster than wooden ones). Wipe the rods with absorbent paper before re-using.

Once all the pastries are fried, prepare the filling. Beat the ricotta until smooth, add the sugar and orange oil, then fold in the chocolate, almonds and candied orange peel.

Using a piping bag with a large plain nozzle, fill the cannoli, and garnish each end with a small piece of candied orange peel.

CARTOCCI

CUSTARD-FILLED HORNS

*Made with sweetened yeast dough, these individual pastries are quite a meal
in themselves. Spirals of pastry are deep-fried and then filled with crema pasticcera.
Traditionally the cartocci are from Sicily, specifically Palermo, where you can still buy them
with the authentic filling of sweetened ricotta.*

*If the idea of making these pastries on rods is too daunting, roll the dough into balls as you
would make doughnuts. Rest to prove, then fry. When cold, fill with crema pasticcera or jam.*

Makes 10 large pastries

30 g (1 oz) fresh yeast or 7 g (¼ oz) dried
½ tablespoon malt (optional)
160 mL (5½ fl oz) cold milk
1 egg
lemon zest
1 tablespoon castor (superfine) sugar
a pinch of salt
375 g (12 oz) plain (all-purpose) flour
1 tablespoon unsalted butter
1 egg
2 tablespoons milk
vegetable oil for frying
1½ recipes Crema Pasticerra (see page 153)
icing (confectioner's) sugar

Soften the yeast and malt in the milk, then stir in the egg, zest, sugar and salt. Mix with the flour to form a dough. Eventually add the butter and knead well.

Place the dough in a large floured bowl and cover with cling wrap. Leave the dough in a warm place (26°C/78°F is ideal) and rest until it has doubled in volume.

Tip the dough onto a floured bench and roll out into a rectangle of approximately 7 mm (⅓ inch) thickness. Cut into strips of pastry 3 cm (1¼ inches) wide.

Combine the egg and milk to make an eggwash. Brush these pastry strips with eggwash and coil them around oiled wooden rods (cannoli rods are suitable). While rolling, the strips should overlap by half and the eggwashed side face outwards to adhere to the coil of pastry, not the rod. Place the 'cartocci' on a tray, and cover with a floured tea-towel as you work. Repeat with the rest of the dough.

Allow the pastries to rest under a cloth to prove slightly.

Heat the oil in a deep pan to a temperature of 175–180°C (350°F). Cook the pastries, two of three at a time, depending on the size of your pan. When cool, remove the rods.

Fit a piping bag with a plain 1 cm (½ inch) tube nozzle and fill the pastries with crema pasticcera. Dust with icing sugar before serving.

LE CROSTATE
THE TARTS

The number and type of Italian tarts are endless, so we have chosen a few favourites based on pasta frolla. Whether you prefer seasonal fruits, homemade jam tarts or are tempted by the apple tart, you will not be disappointed. You'll also find a few cakes in this section.

CROSTATA DI MARMELLATA
JAM TART

Makes 1 × 24 cm (9½ inch) tart

1 recipe Pasta Frolla (see page 152)
1 × 375 g (12 oz) jar jam of your choice
icing (confectioner's) sugar

Preheat the oven to 180°C (350°F).

Prepare the pastry according to the instructions on page 152. Roll out approximately half of the chilled pastry to line a 24 cm (9½ inch) tart case. Press so the pastry sticks to the side. Trim off any excess and reserve. Chill for 20 minutes. Bake blind according to the instructions on page 22. Cool.

Pour the jam into the prepared tart case. Roll out the remaining pastry and, using either a knife or a crinkled edged roller/cutter, cut strips of pastry 1 cm (½ inch) wide and place in a lattice pattern over the jam filling. Carefully cut the excess off at the edges.

Bake at 170°C (330°F) for 30 minutes, checking that the lattice pastry is cooked thoroughly. The jam may be bubbling at this stage. When cool, dust the surface with icing sugar and serve.

CROSTATA DI MANDORLE
ALMOND TART

My favourite memory of enjoying this ubiquitous tart in Italy was during a visit to Venice, where I was invited to a pleasant morning tea at Caffe Florian. The burnished glow of Venetian glass lamps on the faded mirrored walls set the perfect scene. Typically the tart was sublime due to the flavour of the well-roasted nuts. This recipe is not an original, but is easily made and enjoys a moist filling that may be enhanced with additional chopped roasted almonds.

The liquid glucose is optional, and will keep the tart moist.

Makes 1 × 24 cm (9½ inch) tart

PASTRY

1 × 24 cm (9½ inch) tart case lined with Pasta Frolla (see page 152)

icing (confectioner's) sugar

FILLING

100 g (3½ oz) unsalted butter, softened

zest of 1 orange

½ recipe Almond Marzipan Dough Base (see page 155)

1 teaspoon liquid glucose (optional)

2 eggs

130 g (4½ oz) self-raising flour, sifted or 130 g/4½ oz plain (all-purpose) flour and 1 teaspoon baking powder, sifted

40 g (1½ oz) flaked almonds, lightly roasted

Blind bake the pastry in a tin with a removable base according to the instructions on page 22.

Preheat the oven to 170°C (330°F).

To make the filling, cream the butter, zest, almond marzipan and liquid glucose together until a pale yellow colour. Add the eggs, one at a time, mixing well to absorb. Fold in the sifted flour and pour into the prepared tart shell. Sprinkle almonds over the surface and bake for 50 minutes. Allow the tart to cool in the tin.

When cool, transfer to a serving plate and sprinkle with icing sugar.

CROSTATA DI MELA

BAKED APPLE TART

This tart can be eaten hot with cream or ice-cream (gelato) or served at room temperature. It's great for picnics.

Makes 1 × 24 cm (9 ½ inch) tart

1 × 24 cm (9½ inch) tart case lined with Pasta Frolla (see page 152)

5 medium-sized golden delicious or granny smith apples

50 g (1½ oz) unsalted butter

1 vanilla bean (optional)

4 tablespoons honey

a pinch of cinnamon

icing (confectioner's) sugar

Blind bake the pastry in a tin with a removable base according to the instructions on page 22. (The remaining pastry will be used to make the lattice strips.)

Peel, core and quarter the apples.

Melt the butter in a frying pan, then add the split and scraped vanilla bean. Turn the heat to high, and as the butter browns, add the apple pieces, tossing occasionally, allowing them to colour slightly and cook. Spoon over the honey and continue to toss with the cinnamon. This process will take 10–15 minutes. The resulting apples will be partially cooked and caramelised. Allow to cool with the juices.

Preheat the oven to 180°C (350°F).

Place the cold apples and juices in the pre-baked tart case. Cut the remaining Pasta Frolla into strips and use to form a lattice pattern over the apples.

Bake the tart for 35–40 minutes until the lattice pastry is golden and the caramelised honey bubbles around the fruit. Remove from the oven, and dust with icing sugar before serving.

Back: Crostata di Mela;
Front: Crostata di Frutta (see page 178)

CROSTATA DI FRUTTA

FRESH FRUIT TART

Makes 1 × 24 cm (9½ inch) tart

1 × 24 cm (9½ inch) tart case lined with Pasta Frolla (see page 152)

an assortment of fresh fruits; for example, strawberries, bananas, kiwifruit, cherries, raspberries, oranges and apples

½ recipe Crema Pasticcera (see page 153)

1 sachet (30 g/1 oz) commercial jelly glaze

Blind bake the pastry in a tin with a removable base according to the instructions on page 22.

Wash, peel and slice the fruit of your choice.

Spread the *crema pasticcera* in the tart case and smooth the surface. Arrange the fruit in a pretty pattern over the surface. Glaze the fruit with jelly (follow the instructions on the packet/box).

Refrigerate before serving.

CROSTATA DI RICOTTA

ITALIAN RICOTTA CHEESECAKE

Creamy and studded with plump sultanas, this ricotta tart is loved by all who taste it. Using the Pasta Frolla ensures a good crust to support the wet filling, which improves in flavour on the second day. Eat at room temperature for optimum quality.

Makes 1 × 26 cm (10½ inch) cake

1 recipe Pasta Frolla (see page 152)
3 eggs
110 g (3½oz) castor (superfine) sugar
350 g (11½ oz) cream cheese, softened
650 g (1½ lb) ricotta
80 ml (2½ fl oz) cream
80 g (2½ oz) blanched almond meal
80 g (2½ oz) candied orange peel or citron
100 g (3½ oz) sultanas, soaked in rum or brandy
icing (confectioner's) sugar

Preheat the oven to 180°C (350°F).

Cut out a disc of pastry to fit the base of the springform tin and bake on a tray until golden brown, 12–15 minutes. When cold, place the pastry disc into the springform tin with the sides attached. Press the extra, softened dough onto the walls, easing it upwards, and smearing some over the edges of the base to attach. The pastry should be 4–5 mm (¼ inch) thick. Trim the edge approximately 1 cm (½ inch) from the top of the tin to produce a tart wall 5 cm (2 inches) high.

Whisk the eggs and 60 g (2 oz) castor sugar until thick and pale. Set aside.

Beat the cream cheese and the remaining sugar until smooth, then add the ricotta and beat until smooth again.

Add the cream, then gradually add the egg mixture. Mix until all the ingredients are well combined.

Fold in the almond meal, peel and sultanas, and pour the mixture into the prepared base. Bake for 1 hour. The filling rises slightly and is a light golden brown when cooked. Cool in the tin.

When cool, transfer to a serving plate and dust with icing sugar.

TORTA DELIZIOSA

DELICIOUS CAKE

Torta Deliziosa can be found all over Italy, and is distinctive not only in flavour but in presentation as well. It is a sponge cake scented with Maraschino liqueur and garnished with apricot jam and the traditional piped almond paste. The keeping properties of this cake are very good due to the moist centre and the sealed almond surface.

Makes 1 × 20 cm (8 inch) cake

1 × 20 cm (8 inch) Plain Sponge (see page 154)
Light Sugar Syrup (see page 155)
Maraschino liqueur (optional)
smooth apricot jam
candied fruit (optional)

ALMOND PASTE
300 g (10 oz) blanched almond meal
160 g (5 1/2 oz) candied orange peel, diced
250 g (8 oz) castor (superfine) sugar
150 mL (5 fl oz) egg whites (5 egg whites)
125 g (4 oz) icing (confectioner's) sugar

To make the almond paste, lightly roast the almond meal until it begins to turn the palest honey colour. Cool.

In a food processor, blend the orange peel, castor sugar and egg whites until you get a smooth orange mixture. Add the almond meal and blend. Transfer to a bowl and stir in the icing sugar to form a thick, sticky 'paste'. The paste needs to be thick to hold its shape when piping. If too thick, add a little more egg white to soften the mixture.

To assemble the cake, split the sponge in half. Brush the base with a little sugar syrup enhanced with the Maraschino liqueur, and gently spread with a fine layer of the almond paste, taking care not to tear the sponge. Then place on the top layer of sponge. Brush lightly with sugar syrup.

Bring the apricot jam to the boil then carefully brush the entire face of the cake with a very fine layer of the jam to seal the surface. Transfer the cake onto a tray lined with a piece of non-stick baking paper.

Using a corrugated piping tube set into a piping bag, pipe vertical rows of almond paste around the side of the cake, overlapping about 1 cm (1/2 inch) onto the top to the cake. Once this is completed, pipe a basket-weave pattern on top. Allow the cake to stand overnight for the surface to dry a little.

The next day, bake in an oven preheated to 200°C (400°F) for 10–15 minutes — rotate if necessary to avoid any dark patches. The baking seals the almond paste. When the cake is cold, brush it very lightly with boiled apricot jam, and garnish with candied fruit if desired.

This cake is best eaten at room temperature.

LA SFOGLIATA

MANY LEAVES

I wouldn't necessarily wait for a special occasion to contemplate making this! The success of this cake depends on the puff pastry, and how well it is cooked. To maintain a good crunch, the pastry should be a deep golden brown and thoroughly cooked through. Contrary to common presentation, the cake should be made with four layers, though three will suffice. Finish with roasted flaked almonds and a light dusting of icing sugar.

This traditional cake is light and delicious, and often used for birthday celebrations as an alternative to a continental sponge cake.

Makes 1 × 24 cm (9½ inch) cake

3 × 28 cm (11 inch) discs Pasta Sfoglia
(see page 150)
1½ recipes Crema Pasticcera (see page 153)
roasted flaked almonds
icing (confectioner's) sugar

Prick the pastry discs all over with a fork and bake in a preheated oven at 180°C (350°F) for 45–55 minutes. The pastry should be well cooked and a dark honey-brown colour. Trim the pastry discs so that they are a uniform 24 cm (9½ inches).

To assemble, spread a 1–1.5 cm (½ inch) layer of *crema pasticcera* on a layer of pastry. Position the second layer of pastry on top and spread *crema* over the surface. Invert the third layer of pastry and position on top (so that the flat base of the disc becomes the top of the cake and the 'puff' sits on the *crema*). Carefully mask the sides of the cake with any remaining *crema*, taking care not to smear the surface.

Press the flaked almonds onto the side of the cake and dust with icing sugar. Transfer to a serving plate and chill before serving.

DIPLOMATICO

DIPLOMAT'S CAKE

Commonly purchased as a slice, the Diplomatico adapts to a delicious cake to be shared on festive occasions. The distinctive feature and flavour is that of the liqueur Alkermes, which is an aromatic blend of orange peel, cinnamon, mace, vanilla, clove, coriander and cardamom plus the addition of cochineal to provide the striking red colour. Alkermes can be purchased in a concentrated form from specialist continental grocers. It is worth taking the trouble to prepare the pastry by hand rather than substituting pre-prepared pastry. When made correctly, the pastry combined with sponge cake, Alkermes and crema *is light and delicious.*

Makes 1 × 26 cm (10½ inch) cake

2 × 30 cm (12 inch) discs Pasta Sfoglia (see page 150)

1 × 26 cm (10½ inch) disc Plain Sponge (see page 154)

1½ recipes Crema Pasticcera (see page 153)

½ recipe Light Sugar Syrup (see page 155), scented with Alkermes extract

roasted flaked almonds

icing (confectioner's) sugar

Preheat the oven to 180°C (350°F).

Prick the pastry discs and bake in the preheated oven for 45–55 minutes. The pastry should be well cooked and a dark honey-brown colour. Trim the pastry discs so that they are approximately 1 cm (½ inch) larger than the disc of sponge.

To assemble, spread a 1 cm (½ inch) layer of *crema pasticcera* on the first layer of pastry. Place the sponge layer on top. Brush with sufficient syrup to leave the sponge wet but not saturated. Cover with another layer of *crema*. Invert the second layer of pastry and place on top, thus making the surface flat and smooth.

Mask the sides with the remaining *crema* and gently press on the flaked almonds. Dust the top with icing sugar. The cake can be chilled before serving, though it is best eaten at room temperature.

Above: Diplomatico (page 183)
Right: Pastiera Napoletana (page 186)

PASTIERA NAPOLETANA
WHEAT TART FROM NAPLES

La pastiera is a classic tart from Naples, originally made at Easter, though it can now be found year round in its area of origin and in major cities. Bound with ricotta and enhanced with vanilla, citrus peel and cinnamon, this tart has the most delicious flavour and consistency due to its filling of moist wheat grains. It keeps well; in fact the flavour is better the next day.

Makes 1 × 26 cm (10½ inch) tart

1 × 26 cm (10½ inch) tart case lined with Pasta Frolla (see page 152)

125 g (4 oz) whole wheat or 400 g (14 oz) canned cooked wheat (gran pastiera)

500 mL (2 cups/16 fl oz) milk

1 cinnamon stick

1 vanilla bean

zest of 1 lemon

icing (confectioner's) sugar

FILLING

3 egg yolks

50 g (1½ oz) castor (superfine) sugar

300 g (10 oz) ricotta

80 g (2½ oz) candied orange peel, diced

3 egg whites

2 tablespoons castor (superfine) sugar

Blind bake the pastry shell according to the instructions on page 179.

It is worth taking the time to prepare the wheat. Soak the wheat in cold water for 24 hours. The next day, bring a pot of water to the boil with ½ teaspoon salt. Add the wheat and boil for 1 hour. Drain.

In a food processor pulse the wheat to crack open the outer shell (bran). Do not blend to a paste — the wheat should still be in quite large pieces. This enables the wheat to absorb the milk more readily as it cooks.

In a heavy-based pan place the wheat, milk, cinnamon, split and scraped vanilla bean and lemon zest. Cook slowly for 1–1½ hours, until the milk is almost absorbed. Watch the pan and stir occasionally to make sure the mixture does not catch. Cool and refrigerate overnight, or for at least 8 hours to absorb any excess milk, and to allow the flavours to intensify.

The next day, preheat the oven to 180°C (350°F).

To make the filling, whisk together the yolks and sugar. Change to a beater attachment and add the ricotta. Blend well together.

Remove the cinnamon, vanilla bean and zest from the wheat and fold the wheat into the filling with the candied peel.

Whisk the egg whites. When they are foamy and at soft peaks stage, add the 2 tablespoons of castor sugar and continue whisking until firm peaks form. Fold the egg whites through the ricotta/wheat base. Pour the mixture into the prepared base, and spread evenly.

Bake for 50 minutes to 1 hour. The centre should be firm when lightly pressed. When cold, dust with icing sugar. Serve at room temperature.

SPUMA DI MOSCATO CON LAMPONI

MOSCATO ZABAGLIONE WITH RASPBERRIES

They say that a change is as good as a holiday, so why not consider an easy alternative to zabaglione? This froth of Moscato marries well with fresh raspberries and is enhanced with the crunch of crostoli.

Makes 4–6

200 mL (7 fl oz) Moscato (Italian sweet white wine)

4 egg yolks

80 g (2 1/2 oz) castor (superfine) sugar

80 g (2 1/2 oz) raspberries per person (see note)

Crostoli (see page 166) or wafers

Combine the Moscato, yolks and sugar in a stainless steel bowl over a pan of boiling water. Using a balloon whisk, whisk constantly until a pale, thick froth forms. At this stage the spuma will be quite hot.

Fill martini glasses with raspberries, pour over the spuma and garnish with crostoli or wafer biscuits and serve immediately.

NOTE Fruits other than raspberries can be used; other berries work well, as do diced seasonal fruits, especially ripe pears.

ROSA'S PANETTONE CAKE

Who is Rosa, and why is her cake included? Rosa lives down the street from my parents, and always has a little something cooking as she is from the school of true Italian hospitality. We went to school with her children, we all played together and if we were lucky, Rosa had made her cake. We knew this the moment she called up the street. Though it is not the classic yeasted panettone, this cake typifies the glorious simple cakes made by Italian mothers. And surprise, surprise, it is made with olive oil, not butter.

Makes 1 × 24 cm (9½ inch) cake

3 eggs
200 g (7 oz) castor (superfine) sugar
120 mL (4 fl oz) olive oil
120 mL (4 fl oz) milk
zest of 1 lemon
350 g (11½ oz) plain (all-purpose)
or self-raising flour
10 g (⅓ oz) baking powder (omit if using
self-raising flour)
100 g (3½ oz) sultanas
roasted almonds, chopped
castor (superfine) sugar

Preheat the oven 175°C (350°F). Butter and flour a 25 cm (10 inch) cake tin.

Whisk the eggs and sugar until thick and pale. With the mixer on a low speed, gradually pour in the oil, milk and zest.

Sift the flour and baking powder together. Toss the sultanas in a little of the flour, then fold the sifted flour and sultanas into the egg mixture.

Pour into the tin and sprinkle with the almonds and sugar. Bake for 50–60 minutes. The cake rises and is honey coloured when cooked. Test by inserting a skewer in the middle: it should come out clean.

AMORE DI POLENTA

LOVE OF POLENTA

Only the Veneti (folk from the region of Veneto) could be so lyrical about polenta! The use of this coarsely ground maize flour to complete a cake batter will surprise, not only with the resulting colour but with flavour and texture. A drier style of cake is enjoyed for breakfast, morning and afternoon tea; it marries well with a dry or sweeter-style white wine.

Makes 1 × 20 cm (8 inch) cake

75 g (2¹/₂ oz) plain (all-purpose) flour
35 g (1 oz) polenta (cornmeal)
50g (2 oz) fine yellow semolina (see note)
1 teaspoon baking powder
60 g (2 oz) almond meal
125 g (4 oz) unsalted butter
140 g (4¹/₂ oz) castor (superfine) sugar
4 egg yolks
2 eggs
50 g (1¹/₂ oz) fine yellow semolina
extra castor (superfine) sugar

Preheat the oven to 170°C (330°F). Butter and flour a 20 cm (8 inch) round cake tin.

Sift the flour, polenta, semolina, baking powder and almond meal together.

Cream the butter and sugar until light and fluffy. Gradually add the egg yolks and beat until incorporated. Add the eggs, one at a time, and continue beating until the mixture is a pale yellow.

Fold the sifted ingredients through the butter base until just combined. Pour into the prepared tin and smooth the surface. Sprinkle over the yellow semolina and extra sugar.

Bake for 40 minutes until the surface is golden. A skewer inserted into the centre should come out clean.

NOTE If fine yellow semolina is unavailable, use an additional 50g (2 oz) of polenta.

192

A GONDOLA ON THE MURRAY

SAVOIARDI

SPONGE FINGERS

These light sponge fingers are eaten with coffee, dipped into sweetened wine or used as a base for desserts such as tiramisu. These biscuits are also available commercially prepared.

Makes approximately 25 fingers

4 egg yolks
2 tablespoons castor (superfine) sugar
40 g (1 1/4 oz) plain (all-purpose) flour
40 g (1 1/4 oz) cornflour (cornstarch)
4 egg whites
80 g (2 1/2 oz) castor (superfine) sugar
extra castor (superfine) sugar

Preheat the oven to 180°C (350°F).

Whisk the yolks and sugar until thick and pale. Sift the flour and cornflour together.

In a clean bowl, whisk the egg whites to a soft meringue, then gradually add the sugar.

Fold a third of the meringue into the yolks, then fold in the remaining meringue and flours in alternate lots. Mix gently, and stop once the ingredients are combined.

Transfer the mixture into a piping bag fitted with a plain round tube 1 cm (1/2 inch) in diameter.

Pipe the sponge fingers onto strips of non-stick baking paper. Carefully lift the piped biscuits and invert onto a tray filled with castor sugar. Once the surfaces are coated, place on baking trays and bake for 15–25 minutes, depending on the degree of dryness you prefer.

CASSATA

*This is definitely not the traditional cassata; it is, in fact, a parfait recipe that is
enhanced with the flavours of a cassata. Stefano loves to make this recipe because
of the incredible velvety texture, which is imparted by the cooked sugar technique. As a
frozen dessert it can be made beforehand, then sliced to serve and garnished
with fruit or biscuits.*

Yield 1 × 20 cm × 7.5 cm (8 inch × 3 inch) tin

2 eggs

4 egg yolks

180 g (6 oz) castor (superfine) sugar

100 mL (3½ fl oz) water

3 tablespoons Grand Marnier

2 tablespoons lemon juice

zest of 2 lemons

150 g (5 oz) glacé fruits, finely diced

600 mL (1 pint) cream (35% fat),
softly whipped

Whisk the eggs and yolks together.

In a saucepan, combine the sugar and water and heat to 120°C (250°F), soft-ball stage on a candy thermometer. Slowly pour the sugar into the egg mixture, whisking all the time. Continue whisking until the mixture is cool, thick and pale.

Stir in the Grand Marnier, lemon juice and zest, and the glacé fruit. Carefully fold in the whipped cream.

Line the loaf tin with cling wrap, leaving some overhang on the sides.

Pour the mixture into the prepared tin and cover the top with cling wrap to ensure a tight seal. Freeze.

To serve, warm the inverted tin under tepid water to loosen slightly. Remove the plastic and place the cassata on a board or serving dish. Cut the cassata into 1–1.5 cm (½ inch) slices. Garnish with fresh fruit and a wafer biscuit.

196

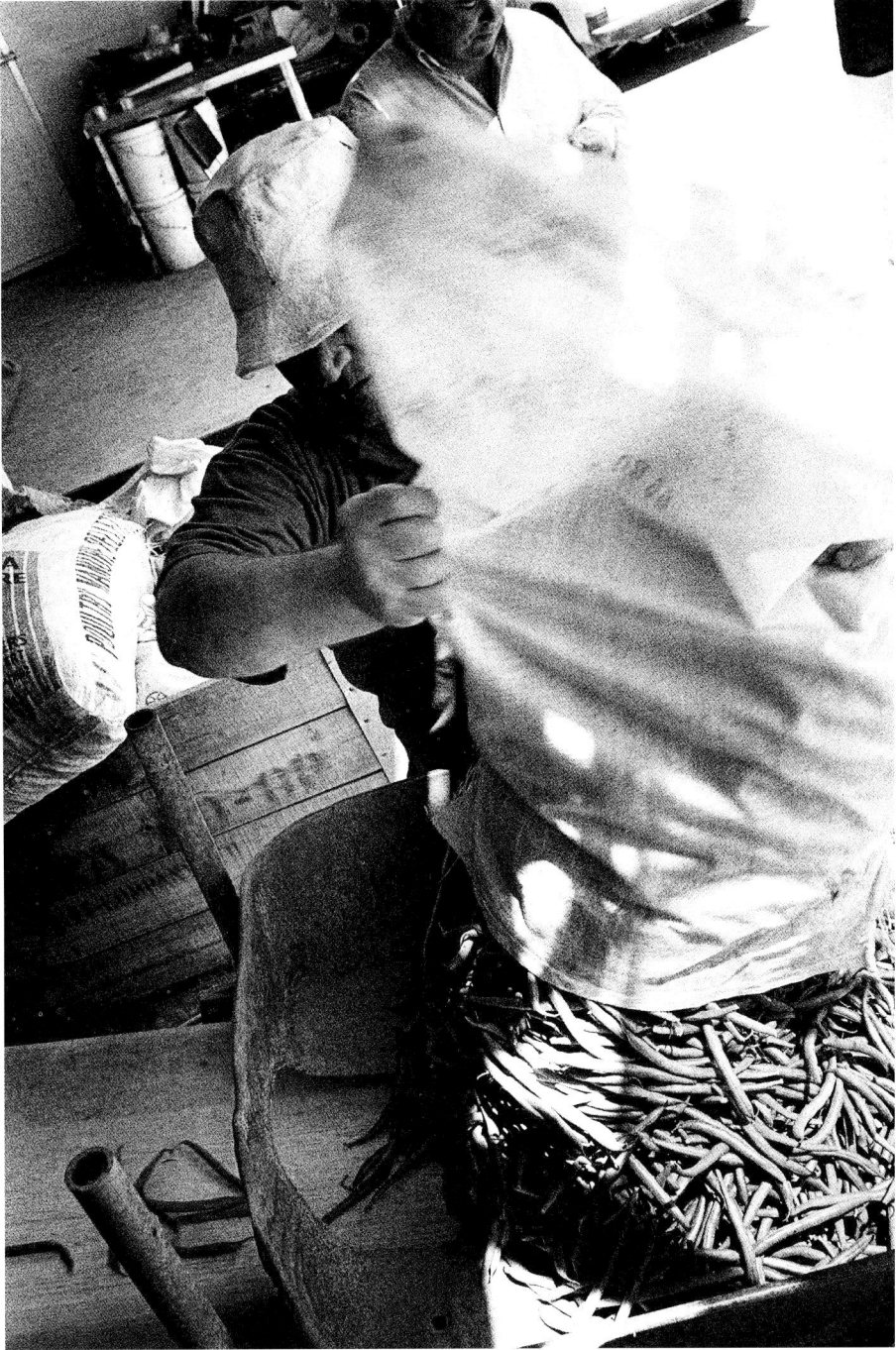

197
A GONDOLA ON THE MURRAY

A NOTE ABOUT SOME INGREDIENTS

First, imported or domestic?

Horses for courses, I say, just keep quality in the forefront of your mind. There are some products that Australia doesn't make very well or cannot make at all — for example, certain types of cheese, pasta, salted capers and dried fish. But use what you can find, and according to how much you want to spend.

ANCHOVIES AND SARDINES

Anchovies are indispensable in Italian cooking, but salted sardines can be used, and they are exceptional. Many dishes that require salty fish are prepared with anchovies.

The slender and tasty fillets of anchovies, while not to everyone's taste, liven up many dishes from salads to pizzas, antipasto to spaghetti. When they find their way into a small and round capsicum with a caper — as they do in Piedmont — they elevate this morsel of food to great heights. Anchovies travel well with boiled potatoes and tomatoes. Put tomatoes, potatoes, green beans and anchovies in the same bowl, and add, for argument's sake, olives, garlic, chillies and olive oil and you will notice that anchovies are so accommodating that they agree with everything.

So much for anchovies. Confusion arises when a recipe specifies salted sardines rather than anchovies, or when the word 'anchovy' is unintentionally used instead of salted sardines.

Sardines usually come fresh, frozen, or in cans with oil. In continental shops, however, they can be found preserved in salt inside giant, colourful tins. These are used for certain preparations that rely on their exceptional flavour. (Anchovies also come preserved in the same fashion but are more expensive.) But the shopkeepers I spoke to were quick to point out that many consumers preferred the salted sardines to the anchovies.

Most consumers, however, remain ignorant of sardines. This is a pity because it precludes them from special dishes enjoyed in the Mediterranean for centuries. Salted sardines need to have their salt removed by rinsing under a tap for a little while. The fillets then have to be carefully stripped of bones (the odd remaining bone will disappear during the cooking process).

When combined with butter, sardine fillets are reminiscent of another fish product called bottarga: fish eggs preserved in salt. Bottarga is much, much more complex, but then it is much, much more expensive. I regard salted sardine as the bottarga of the poor.

BUTTER

Pastry cooks always use 'unsalted' butter and will enhance flavours with salt. This 'sweet' butter is available at supermarkets and lends itself better to cake and pastry-making.

CAPERS

The ones in vinegar have a limited use. Squeeze out the vinegar, because it is usually too strong. The salted capers from Southern Italy are really easy to handle. Wash away the salt in several changes of water and taste as you go. Do not overwash or soak for too long, or you kill the soul of this special condiment. Dry the capers on a tea-towel, place in a jar and cover with olive oil. Use as you need.

CHEESE, PARMESAN

The best parmigiano is expensive, but can be used with extreme moderation. Again, good parmesan is a product of time and patience.

Grana padano is slightly cheaper, and excellent in some cases. When I say parmesan, I refer to a style of cheese. You check your pocket and see which one you can afford. If all you can afford is a locally made grated cheese called parmesan, so be it, as long as it is not sawdust.

Sometimes I specify pecorino, because it is saltier and more suited to Southern Italian recipes. There are Australian versions of pecorino.

EGGS

The freshest eggs give the best results. 'Free-range' and 'organic' are more flavoursome and these are our preference. Always use eggs at room temperature as they will absorb into mixes more readily and hold more aeration. If your eggs come directly from the refrigerator, warm them by placing them in a bowl of hot water before using. All eggs used in the sweets section are 55 g (2 1/2 oz).

FLOUR

All the recipes are based on plain flour, which is readily available. Self-raising flour is plain flour that has been commercially prepared with the addition of aeration chemicals. For recipes that state plain flour and baking powder you can substitute both ingredients with the flour weight in self-raising flour (and omit the baking powder). For recipes that list plain flour do not substitute self-raising flour.

GARLIC

I have been asked many times what I think of chopped garlic preserved in oil. I do not like it. I like to fiddle as little as possible with garlic. It is best to chop it or crush it and use it immediately.

If left for too long garlic becomes stinky and oxidised. Sometimes I prefer putting a whole clove into what I am cooking and taking it out later.

Loads of garlic are kept in the coolroom for too long, which will turn it green. Take it back and ask for a refund. When it is yellow and transparent like a lolly, it stinks. Get a refund as well. There is nothing worse than imperfect garlic.

NUTS

Nuts are highly perishable due to their oil content, which will eventually become rancid. It is best to buy the freshest available from vendors who turn over stock regularly. Purchase in larger quantities and freeze them, regardless of type or how the nut is processed.

OIL, OLIVE

Prepare food as much as possible with extra-virgin olive oil. I fry with plain olive oil. Sometimes I feel that an extra-virgin oil would be too strong, particularly when I am cooking with Asian ingredients.

OILS, FLAVOURED

There are many flavoured oils around these days, including the notorious truffle oil. Many of us have succumbed to the temptation to use this oil here and there. You must be careful, because it is overpowering. Many brands display what I call a synthetic flavour, a whiff of chemicals that I find unappetising. Porcini oils — oils infused with the flavour of porcini mushroom — seem also to fall under this category.

Various agrumato — oils with a citrus content, be it tangerine, lemon or orange — can be tricky. One drop too many, and you end up with a citrus grove on your plate, so use them sparingly.

ONIONS

I prefer to use the yellow variety. Some fresh ones in spring are also nice. Shallots — not spring onions (green onions or scallions) — do give great results, but you have to put some effort into it. You can replace all onions with shallots if you like.

PARSLEY, ITALIAN

I do not like chopping parsley; it can easily turn to hay in flavour. Break it with your hands over the food at the most appropriate time, usually at the end, when the food is ready to be served.

POLENTA

Australian polenta is a model of efficiency. It cooks quickly, although sometimes I find it lacking somewhat in flavour. Make up your own mind, but to do so you have to make an effort and go looking for some different stuff, say, with the flour ground to a different thickness, a different colour of flour, or mixed with other ingredients.

POTS AND PANS

Not an ingredient, but indispensible. No-one in my family sells them, so I am beyond suspicion when I declare my enthusiasm for Bessemer pots and pans. These are non-stick, great heat distributors, and ideal for long braising or cooking. They are eternal if you look after them and I believe they are Australian made, which is even more pleasing.

SALT AND OTHER SEASONING

A doctor friend told me that salt is salt and it can all be equally bad for you. He may be right. But when I taste salt from Sicily or from England or France I detect a difference in flavour. Have a go and check it out for yourself.

The pepper grinder is useful, even though black pepper does not look good on white fish.

For me, chillies are another form of seasoning, as are Thai fish sauce, anchovies, truffle oil and soy sauce. Many of these products contain salt as an integral part of their distinctive flavour. Hence, instead of just salt, one of these may be enough to add complexity to food.

In this book I write 'season to taste', which means to season as you like it. There is no point in telling you something so personal and variable. In seasoning, remember that a lot of dried spices are just that — dried and tasteless.

SPICES

As with nuts, choose a vendor who turns over stock regularly. Purchase in small quantities rather than storing milled spices for long periods, which will result in loss of pungency.

SUGAR

Castor (superfine) sugar is suited to baking as it is finely milled, thus making it easier to be absorbed into batters and mixes. Regular graded sugar (A1) can be substituted but this will result in spotting on the surfaces and a grainy cake crumb.

VINEGAR, BALSAMIC

A wonderful vinegar, balsamic has become something that tries to be all things to all people. Take it easy and look hard, because some are terrible. Extra-virgin olive oil can be ruined by bad balsamic vinegar. I suggest that a good red-wine vinegar may be better most of the time. Balsamic vinegar takes years to develop — you cannot buy it for $5 and expect it to be good.

SdP

INDEX